# DIARY OF
# A VERY
# BAD
# YEAR

DIARY OF
A VERY
BAD
YEAR

HARPER ⬤ PERENNIAL

NEW YORK • LONDON • TORONTO • SYDNEY • NEW DELHI • AUCKLAND

# DIARY OF A VERY BAD YEAR

## CONFESSIONS OF AN ANONYMOUS HEDGE FUND MANAGER

with *n+1*

Introduction by Keith Gessen

This book would not have happened without the relentless team of *n+1* transcribers: Sarah Davis, Atossa Abrahamian, Edward Morgan Day Frank, Avner Davis, Juli Weiner, and Willa Cmiel. Our gratitude also to Dayna Tortorici for her sharp vision.

HARPER ● PERENNIAL

HarperCollins books may be purchased for educational, business, or sales promotional use. For information, please e-mail the Special Markets Department at SPsales@harpercollins.com.

FIRST EDITION

*Designed by Justin Dodd*

Library of Congress Cataloging-in-Publication Data
    Diary of a very bad year : confessions of an anonymous hedge fund manager / by Anonymous Hedge Fund Manager, [introduction by] Keith Gessen. — 1st ed.
      p.  cm.
    Summary: "A profoundly candid and captivating account of the economic crisis, from an anonymous hedge fund manager"— Provided by publisher.
    ISBN 978-0-06-196530-2 (pbk.)
    1. Hedge funds—Management. 2. Subprime mortgage loans. 3. Global Financial Crisis, 2008–2009. I. Gessen, Keith.
HG4530.D53 2010
332.64'524—dc22                                      2010005728

HB 03.13.2023

# CONTENTS

*Introduction*  vii

## BEFORE THE COLLAPSE

### I. Primetime for Subprime  5
Currency crosses—Black boxes—Death of an expert

### II. The Death of Bear  25
At the office—Run on Bear—Argentina—Night thoughts of an
HFM—Zombie banks—Florida

### III. On the Eve  49
World loves dollars—Fannie & Freddie—How bad is it really?
—Why banks hate bankruptcy—An existential question

## THE COLLAPSE

### IV. How Bad Is It?  67
Death of Lehman and shame of the Reserve Primary Fund—
Central banks respond—AIG bailout—Effects on real economy—
Trading with Martians—The price of bread—Terrifying moments

### V. Year-End Closing 91
Layoffs—Detroit in trouble—Human Resources—Problems with TARP—HFM in Obama administration?—HFM as regulator—Madoff—Obama's stimulus, HFM's concerns

## AFTERMATH
### VI. Populist Rage 125
Visit to China—Dollar as a reserve currency—Is Citi a zombie? —Goldman runs everything—$n+1$ demands an accounting—HFM announces mini-sabbatical

### VII. Life After the Crisis 155
HFM fixes toilets, duns debtors—Missed opportunities—Smash it up!—The fate of the tallest building in Europe—Brazilian meat-packers—Stress tests—More on Obama—HFM's regrets

### VIII. Vacation Plans 181
Memories of Rome—Crime and punishment—150 Years—Things looking up, for Wall St.—Long-Term Capital Management (or, what happens to failed HFMs)—The end of investment banks as we know them

### IX. Farewell 209
California ghost towns—Unemployment—Return of the low-margin bankers—Bullies and betrayers—Harvard blows up a hedge fund—Tears for fears—A shocking announcement

*Epilogue* 249
*Bibliography* 251
*Index* 254

# INTRODUCTION

The anonymous hedge fund manager (HFM) in this book is a friend
of a friend who was introduced to me in late 2006 as a "financial
genius" who ran the emerging markets desk at a respected midtown
fund. I was a little skeptical. I'd been to college with a great many
people who later went into finance, but this was mostly so they could
keep working a lot and drinking beer and watching football afterward.
HFM was not like these folks at all. Finance was not a social event but
an intellectual vocation for him; he spoke quickly, often too quickly
to follow, and told very funny stories about the world he was in. When
the first news about the financial meltdown started appearing in the
nonfinancial press, I asked him for an interview, to see if he could ex-
plain it to me, and on a Sunday afternoon in late September 2007 we
sat down outside a coffee shop in Brooklyn and spoke for two hours
about subprime mortgages, paradigm shifts in finance, the problem
with expertise, and the recent troubles with black box trading systems.
I was an educated American male in my early thirties who lived in
New York and I'd never heard of any of this stuff.

It took me a long time to transcribe the tapes, partly because there
was a lot to do but also because I was worried that the interview hadn't
worked out and I'd wasted HFM's time. I had been entertained when

talking to him, but there wasn't that moment of personal revelation that you get used to waiting for in an interview, if you've done enough journalism. When the transcript was finally finished, I read it through and was amazed. HFM had explained the causes of the crisis with a clarity—and a granularity, a specificity—that I hadn't seen anywhere else. There wasn't a single moment of revelation, because he spoke in entire thoughts, in entire stories; in a way, the whole thing was a revelation. We posted the interview to the website of our magazine, n+1, in part because we thought people in the literary community— n+1 is mostly a literary magazine—would be interested to hear how a financial professional viewed the economic situation. We were right about that. But we didn't anticipate how many business-oriented sites would link to and quote from the interviews. The lucidity of HFM's thinking on these subjects was as new to them as it was to us.

HFM and I sat down for another interview in March 2008, after the collapse of Bear Stearns. Once again HFM discussed the financial situation, but he also let his mind roam freely over the other things he was worried about—the television set on the trading floor at the hedge fund, the Argentinian pots-and-pans bank run of 1998, the state of hedge funds generally. For the second interview I asked one of our interns to transcribe it over the weekend, and we had it up by Monday. A few weeks later we got a report from a friend in business school who said he'd arrived at lecture one day to find that the professor had put two quotes on his blackboard: one from Alan Greenspan, and one from HFM.

The next interview we did was in September 2008, just days before the Lehman bankruptcy sent markets into shock. Since then, we've done one interview every two months, on average. Each time, HFM told me something I didn't know or hadn't thought about; he also told me that he was beginning to experience doubts about the industry he was working in.

+ + +

In going through the transcripts now, a number of things surprise me. One is the tireless magnificence of HFM—he never stops thinking, never stops turning ideas, concepts, and new facts over in his mind. He is, in a sense, dogmatic—it is the dogma of the market, that the efficiency of the market is always going to lead to the best result for everyone—but not in a way that won't allow new information in. As the crisis deepens, he sees the behavior of banks who would pull his financing; as it begins to recede, he sees the way that banks have returned to asking for low margin against risk, because even though it exposes them to danger, the salesman will collect his commission today and someone else will deal with the consequences tomorrow; he sees the way the financial community has dusted itself off and gone back to business as usual. And he draws his conclusions. He sees how things are going, and in certain instances he changes his mind. That a mind so excellent, so generous, so curious, should spend all its time on relative value trading in foreign jurisdictions and yelling at people who refuse to pay him back—well, as HFM says, that is a philosophical question, and beyond the purview of the mere bond market. But it's a philosophical question he begins to tackle on the far side of the crisis, in interviews 7, 8, and 9.

Another thing I notice, reading over these sessions, is that the interviewer (me) is shockingly and embarrassingly ill-informed. I consider myself a person of the left, which means in part that I consider economics to be a prime factor in human life. In fact, I consider a lot of what we think of as human life, as "news," things such as politics and culture, to be determined by economics. But I know almost nothing of economics. I don't think this should disqualify me from membership in the left—I don't consider it the obligation of all good-hearted people to know what a credit default swap is, unless they want to—but let's just say that my ignorance is part of this particular document, and I've left it intact. I know a little more now than when I began, and I realize I should have pressed harder on some of these questions. But as I say, by the end of the interviews HFM began to press on some of them himself.

+ + +

Finally, I should admit a personal interest. At the beginning of the property boom (around 2003), a dear friend of mine ran into some financial trouble—his business foundered and he lost his source of income. All he had (in addition to his beautiful family) was a beautiful house, in a good location, and he borrowed against it, hoping that things would turn around. He took a home equity loan, or line of credit—a HELOC, the ugliest and most ominous of all the ugly acronyms that the crisis gave birth to. My friend could take the HELOC because the house, like everyone else's, was rapidly appreciating. Why sit on that money? He and his family began to live on it while he looked for work. When home prices began to level off in 2005–6 and then finally to plummet, that loan turned into a bad idea. My friend was in trouble. I wanted HFM to help me figure out what would happen to him.

Another thing that happened while we were doing the interviews, a much more terrible thing, was that a friend's uncle, who'd been involved in mortgage brokering and had gone bust the way many of the mortgage brokers did, committed suicide. This was in the summer of 2008, after the housing market had collapsed but before the consequences had reached the broader, "real" economy.

These were stories that took place, as HFM would say, on the margin. During the crisis, there were enough of these stories—for the subprime mortgages had been bundled together into bonds, which were sold off to investment banks, which sold them off to European banks, which sold them to their customers—that they migrated to the center of American life. Now, as the crisis wanes—or at least, with the damage done, news of it wanes—these stories of despair have receded again to the margins. As the billionaire investor Sam Zell said of the many poor people who were given home loans so that the loan originators could make money by selling them to Wall Street, "Those people should go back where they came from." They're going. But the consequences of the years of subprime lending and securitization, of too-easy money and greed and all the vices it gave birth to, will be felt for a long time—not just in the disappearance and reform of some of the Wall Street banks that foolishly put money on those loans, and not just in the battering that ordinary people's retirement savings took in the stock market, but in an increase in inequality.

These interviews for me were profoundly enlightening and interesting, and I have left them substantially intact: We've cut out some boring parts and unnecessary repetitions but have kept the interviews in their proper order, and where HFM was sometimes too optimistic, a little callous, or just off base, we've kept that too. The interviews span two years, from the first rumblings of the crisis in the fall of 2007 to the late summer of 2009, when, at least in the financial markets, the worst had passed, although HFM was apprehensive about another correction. During the final edit HFM went through and added some clarifying footnotes, to keep the information as current as possible.

In the end, though, HFM could not tell me what would happen to my friend who was in danger of losing his house. No one can say what will happen. So while this book offers what I think is an absolutely unprecedented view of what goes on at the very heights of our financial system—it's not so much a world of backslapping, hard-charging, ruthless bankers yelling at each other over speakerphone as a place where the best of human reason, science, and intuition are applied to the question of whether credit spreads will widen or tighten in the next twenty-four hours—it also offers something I consider a bit more hopeful: a portrait of a mind at home in the world, moving with agility and certainty, though not without doubt, not without regret, and not without making its share of mistakes.

Keith Gessen
Brooklyn, New York
October 2009

# BEFORE THE COLLAPSE

The roots of the crisis go back to the aftermath of the Internet bubble correction of 2000 and the terrorist attacks of September 11, 2001. In their wake, to prevent a deepening recession, the Federal Reserve cut interest rates to historic lows—in mid-2003, to 1 percent. This meant that holding money in a bank or in Treasury bills was expensive, whereas getting a loan was cheap. It was especially cheap to get a housing loan. And the federal government, starting with the Clinton administration, had been pushing aggressively for the extension of home loans to as many people as possible.

That was the domestic story. In China during these years a fantastic economic boom was under way, accompanied by a government policy of high savings and no consumption. Chinese workers were paid very little; the government took the profits and invested them in American Treasury bills, bonds, and stocks. China's savings, in other words, were parked in the United States, and it was incumbent on us to spend them. As the housing market took off, spurred on by the laughably low interest rate and the liquidity subsidized by the Chinese, it created a lot of what Wall Street people call "paper." And where there is paper, there can be trades. Innovators at the large investment banks figured out a way to turn all the new mortgages, both good and bad, into bonds, then sell those off. The assets securing the bonds were the houses—which got more and more valuable every month. Parts of California and Florida in particular were in the midst of a building frenzy. Speculators were buying unbuilt property in Florida from developers, then selling it online to other buyers—all before ground had even been broken for the building. The country swarmed with an army of mortgage brokers selling mortgages to whomever they could find and a brigade of developers dutifully putting up the houses those mortgages had bought.

In mid-2005, in response to a glutted housing market, median home prices in the United States finally began to decline. This was, properly speaking, the beginning of the crisis. But it first hit the news in July 2007, when two Bear Stearns hedge funds that had invested heavily in mortgage-backed securities went under.

At this point, two separate but related problems became visible. The first was that holders of subprime mortgages—mortgages extended to people with poor credit, often with no down payment, and often with tricky or adjustable terms—were going to start defaulting at higher-than-predicted rates, and this would obviously have consequences for the people defaulting. The second was that the owner of those mortgages was no longer the original lender: the lenders had bundled the mortgages with other mortgages and sold them off to banks and hedge funds such as the ones at Bear Stearns. The question was whether the problem could be contained. In late August President George W. Bush held a press conference with the secretary of the treasury, Henry Paulson, to assure Americans that homeowners would not be left defenseless and, more important, that the housing (and mortgage) crisis could be isolated. The overall economy "will remain strong enough to weather any turbulence," Bush said, "The recent disturbances in the subprime mortgage industry are modest—they're modest in relation to the size of our economy."

As the Financial Times's Gillian Tett writes, Bush was then asked a follow-up question:

> "Sir, what about the hedge funds and banks that are overexposed on the subprime market? That's a bigger problem! Have you got a plan?"
>
> Bush blinked vaguely. "Thank you!" he said, and then he and Paulson turned to leave.

Our first interview took place a month later on a Sunday afternoon in a coffee shop in Brooklyn.

# HFM I
# PRIME TIME FOR SUBPRIME

*September 30, 2007*
Dow Jones Industrial Average: 13,895.63
Liquid Universe Corporate Index Spread over Benchmark*: 136
U.S. OTR ten-year†: 4.58 percent
Unemployment rate: 4.7 percent
Number of foreclosure filings (previous month): 243,947

**n+1:** Would you like something?

**HFM:** Just a water.

**n+1:** Bottled water? It's on me.

**HFM:** Just tap water, thank you.

---

\* The Credit Suisse metric Liquid Universe Corporate Index Spread over Benchmark is a measure of the difference in yield of an index of liquid U.S. corporate bonds over their benchmark—i.e., the credit spread, which grows when things are volatile (because there's some chance bonds won't be honored) and narrows again when things are calm. Reported in basis points.

† Yield on the generic over-the-counter ten-year U.S. Treasury bond. This is set by the Federal Reserve. When the economy is moving along nicely, the rate tends be around 3 or 4 percent; when the economy overheats, it goes up, to discourage too much lending.

**n+1:** No, really, it's on me.

**HFM:** Thanks, I'm okay.

**n+1:** All right, let's get to it. Is America now a Third World country?

**HFM:** No, we're a First World country with a weak currency. From time to time the dollar's been very weak; from time to time it's very strong; and unfortunately what tends to happen is people tend to just extrapolate. But in reality, over the very long term, currency processes tend to be fairly stable and mean-reverting. So the dollar's very weak today, but that's no reason to believe the dollar's going to be weak forever or that, because it's weak today, it's going to get dramatically weaker tomorrow.*

**n+1:** But you, in your work, are not dealing with the long term . . .

**HFM:** No, we're dealing with the short term. But, I'll tell you, in our work we don't trade the G-7 crosses because we just don't feel we have an edge on that. Dollar-sterling, dollar-euro, or dollar-yen—it's amazing how many brilliant investors have gotten so much egg on their face trying to trade the G-7 crosses. I can think of so many examples where people make these really strong calls that seem very sensible, and then get killed. A very good example of that is Julian Robertson in the late nineties being short the yen against the dollar. Japan had just gone through this horrible deflation, the economy was in the shitter, the banking system was rotten. And all these things you would argue should lead a currency to trade weaker, and he got very, very long the dollar, short the yen, and a lot of people did alongside him, and basically there was a two- or three-week period

---

* DXY, which represents the level of the U.S. dollar against six major world currencies, sat at 77.9 at this time. Over the course of the interviews, it got as high as 88.5 and as low as 71.66. As of the last interview it sat at 76.8, not far from where it started.

in '98 when we had the financial crisis and the yen actually strengthened 10 or 15 percent. I can't remember the exact numbers, but all these guys just got carried out, even though the stylized facts of the argument were very good.*

**n+1:** "Carried out"—is that a term of art?

**HFM:** Carried out . . . like basically they're carried out on a board, they're dead.

Another example of that, a personal example: Generally every year, at the beginning of the year, banks that we deal with will often have events, dinners or lunches, where they gather some of their big clients and discuss themes for the coming year, trade ideas for the coming year. They encourage everybody to, you know, go around the table: "What's your best trade idea for the coming year?" And at the beginning of 2005 I was at a dinner, and I was with some fairly prominent macro investors, and it was almost like a bidding war for who could be more bearish on the dollar. So the first guy would say, "I think the best trade is short dollar, long euro, it's going up to $1.45." At the time, I forget, maybe it was $1.30. And the next guy would go, "No, no, you're so naive. $1.45? It's going to $1.60!" And it was a competition for who could be more bearish on the dollar and win the prize and be the least naive person at the table. "It's going to $1.65 and probably higher! Maybe $1.75!" At the eighteen-month horizon.

Now, considering that everyone at the table being super-bearish on the dollar probably meant that they were already short the dollar and long the euro, I went back and basically looked at my portfolio and said: "Any position I have that's euro-bullish and dollar-bearish, I'm going to reverse it, because if everybody already has said 'I hate the dollar,' they've already positioned for it, who's left?" Who's left to actually make this move happen? And who's on

---

* From October 2, 1998, to October 19, 1998, the dollar-yen rate moved from 135.5 to 114.4.

the other side of that trade? On the other side of the trade is the official sector that has all sorts of other incentives, nonfinancial incentives, political incentives. They want to keep their currency weak to promote growth or exports or jobs. Or they have pegs, peg regimes, that they need to defend, and they don't really care about maximizing profit on their reserves. They're not a bank trying to maximize profits, they have broad policy objectives—and infinite firepower.

**n+1:** So you did well.

**HFM:** We didn't lose. I mean, I don't bet on this process, but sometimes there are other positions you have on that you can say have a certain derivative exposure to the dollar-euro, and we tried to be careful not to take too much of that. Because we thought that this consensus, this superstrong consensus that the dollar's got to go weaker, actually represented a risk that the dollar would go in the other direction.

**+ + +**

**n+1:** How do you know all this stuff?

**HFM:** How do I know all what stuff?

**n+1:** All the stuff that you know. Did you go to—

**HFM:** I didn't go to business school. I did not major in economics. I learned the old-fashioned way, by apprenticing to a very talented investor, so I wound up getting into the hedge fund business before I think many people knew what a hedge fund was. I've been doing it for over ten years. I'm sure today I would never get hired.

**n+1:** Really?

**HFM:** Yeah, it would be impossible because I had no background, or I had a very exiguous background in finance. The guy who hired me always talked about hiring good intellectual athletes, people who were sort of mentally agile in an all-around way, and that the specifics of finance you could learn, which I think is true. But at the time, I mean, no hedge fund was really flooded with applicants, and that allowed him to let his mind range a little bit and consider different kinds of candidates. Today we have a recruiting group, and what do they do? They throw résumés at you, and it's, like, one business school guy, one finance major after another, kids who, from the time they were twelve years old, were watching Jim Cramer and dreaming of working in a hedge fund. And I think in reality that probably they're less likely to make good investors than people with sort of more interesting backgrounds.

**n+1:** Why?

**HFM:** Because I think that in the end the way that you make a ton of money is calling paradigm shifts, and people who are real finance types, maybe they can work really well within the paradigm of a particular kind of market or a particular set of rules of the game—and you can make money doing that—but the people who make huge money, the George Soroses and Julian Robertsons of the world, they're the people who can step back and see when the paradigm is going to shift, and I think that comes from having a broader experience, a little bit of a different approach to how you think about things.

**n+1:** What's a paradigm shift in finance?

**HFM:** Well, a paradigm shift in finance is maybe what we've gone through in the subprime market and the spillover that's had in a lot of other markets where there were really basic assumptions that people made that—you know what?—they were wrong.

The thing is that nobody has enough brainpower to question every assumption, to think about every single facet of an investment. There are certain things you need to take for granted. And people would take for granted the idea that, "Okay, something that Moody's rates triple-A must be money-good, so I'm going to worry about the other things I'm investing in, but when it comes time to say, 'Where am I going to put my cash?' I'll just leave it in triple-A commercial paper; I don't have time to think about everything." It could be the case that, yeah, the power's going to fail in my office, and maybe the water supply is going to fail, and I should plan for that, but you only have so much brainpower, so you think about what you think are the relevant factors, the factors that are likely to change. But often some of those assumptions that you make are wrong.

**n+1:** So the Moody's ratings were like the water running . . .

**HFM:** Exactly. Triple-A is triple-A. But there were people who made a ton of money in the subprime crisis because they looked at the collateral that underlay a lot of these CDOs [collateralized debt obligations] and commercial paper programs that were highly rated and they said, "Wait a second. What's underlying this are loans that have been made to people who really shouldn't own houses—they're not financially prepared to own houses. The underwriting standards are materially worse than they've been in previous years; the amount of construction that's going on in particular markets is just totally out of proportion with the sort of household formation that's going on; the rating agencies are kind of asleep at the switch, they're not changing their assumptions, and therefore, okay, notwithstanding something may be rated triple-A, I can come up with what I think is a realistic scenario where those securities are impaired." And pricing on triple-A CDO paper was very, very rich. Spreads were very, very tight, and these guys said, "You know what? These assumptions that triple-A is money-good, or the assumptions that underlay Moody's ratings . . . "

**n+1:** Money-good?

**HFM:** In other words, if you buy a bond, you're going to get back your principal. It's money-good. You're going to get 100 cents on the dollar back.

But in reality this was wrong, and people were able to short triple-A securities very cheaply. They weren't paying a lot to be short and they made huge money on triple-A securities and triple-A CDO paper that now trades at 50 cents on the dollar. I mean, that is like the water's not running today, right? *The sun didn't rise.* But if you were trained in finance, you probably are more likely to take for granted that, you know, "The rating agencies have a very sound process, credit analysis, the same process that I've been trained in, all the assumptions that I use are kind of the same as the assumptions they use." In the same fashion, if you assess the attractiveness of a trade based on historical data from a time when people weren't really actively doing that trade, and then suddenly everybody's doing that trade, the behavior of the trade will be different. And if you're trained the same way as everybody else, in general you're all going to behave the same. And when everyone behaves the same, that makes trades a lot riskier: everybody's buying at the same time, you get bubbles, everybody's selling at the same time, you get crashes.

A good example of that is . . . I don't know if you've heard about the problems that cropped up over the summer in a type of business called statistical arbitrage, stat arb?

**n+1:**

**HFM:** Quantitative trading?

**n+1:**

**HFM:** Goldman Sachs had a fund that lost 30 percent, and High-bridge had a fund that lost a lot of money. Stat arb is, basically, computerized trading of a huge universe of stocks based on a set of models. And those models can be technical models like momentum or mean reversion, or it can be based on fundamental models like just "Buy stocks that have high cash-flow yields and sell stocks that have low cash-flow yields." That's a gross simplification, but the core of it is the idea that there are certain predictable relationships between either stock price history and future performance or fundamental variables of a company and stock price performance, and these are broadly reliable. It's not like any given stock is going to perform in line with the models. But if you're trading a universe of five thousand stocks, in general you'll have enough of an edge that you'll make money.

**n+1:** And so the computers themselves are making these trades?

**HFM:** You build the models and the computer does the trading. You actually do all the analysis. But it's too many stocks for a human brain to handle, so it's really just guys with a lot of physics and hard-core statistics backgrounds who come up with ideas about models that might lead to excess return, and then they test them, and then basically all these models get incorporated into a bigger system that trades stocks in an automated way.

**n+1:** So the computers are running the . . .

**HFM:** Yeah, the computer is sending out the orders and doing the trading.

**n+1:** It's just a couple steps from that to the computers enslaving—

**HFM:** Yes, but I for one welcome our computer trading masters.

People actually call it "black box trading," because sometimes you don't even know why the black box is doing what it's doing, because the whole idea is that if you could, you should be doing it yourself. But it's something that's done on such a big scale, a universe of several thousand stocks, that a human brain can't do it in real time. The problem is that the DNA of a lot of these models is very, very similar, it's like an ecosystem with no biodiversity, because most of the people who do stat arb can trace their lineage, their intellectual lineage, back to four or five guys who really started the whole black box trading discipline in the seventies and eighties. And what happened is, in August, a few of these funds that have big black box trading books suffered losses in other businesses and they decided to reduce risk, so they basically dialed down the black box system. So the black box system started unwinding its positions, and every black box is so similar that everybody was kind of long the same stocks and short the same stocks. So when one fund starts selling off its longs and buying back its shorts, that causes losses for the next black box, and the people who run that black box say, "Oh gosh! I'm losing a lot more money than I thought I could. My risk model is no longer relevant; let me turn down my black box." And basically what you had was an avalanche where everybody's black box is being shut off, causing incredibly bizarre behavior in the market.

**n+1:** By the black boxes?

**HFM:** Well, in the part of the profit-and-loss that they were generating to the point where, to give you an example from our black box system, because we have one . . .

**n+1:** A big black box?

**HFM:** Actually I think it's gray, and it's not in our main office, it's off-site. And we made sure it has no arms or legs or anything it could use to enslave us. But we had a loss over the course of three days that was like a ten-sigma event, meaning, you know, it should never happen based on the statistical models that underlie it. Because the model doesn't assume that everybody else is trading the same model as you are. So that's sort of like a meta-model factor. The model doesn't know that there are other black boxes out there.

**n+1:** What's a ten-sigma event?

**HFM:** Meaning that it's ten standard deviations from the mean . . . meaning it's basically impossible, you know? But it's kind of a joke, because returns are very fat-tailed, so the joke that we always say is, "Oh my God, today I had a loss that's a six-sigma event! I mean, that's the first time that's happened in three months!" It's like a one-in-ten-thousand-year event, and I haven't had one in the last three months.

**+ + +**

**n+1:** So why did all of the hedge funds have this subprime mortgage paper?

**HFM:** Well, some hedge funds did and some didn't. Some hedge funds made a lot of money being short it. Some hedge funds lost money being long it. Where the losses are concentrated, though, are not so much in the hedge fund world. The losses are concentrated at banks . . . a lot of European banks, Asian banks. Even the Chinese central bank has exposure.

So it's kind of interesting, people talked about this being a hedge fund problem, but it wasn't really a hedge fund problem. There were some hedge funds that were in the business of taking pure subprime exposure, but most hedge funds, what they were doing is sort of like the CDO business, so what they would do is buy all sorts of mortgage pools. They buy mortgages, and then they package them and they tranche the pools of mortgages up into various tranches from senior to equity. So basically you have a number of tranches of paper that get issued that are backed by the mortgage pools and there's a cash flow waterfall, the cash comes in from those mortgages, a certain tranche has the first priority. And then you have descending order of priority, and the hedge fund would usually keep the last piece, which is known as the equity, or the residual, as opposed to the stuff that was triple-A, that's the most senior paper. So if you had a pool of half a billion dollars of mortgages, maybe there would be $300 million of triple-A paper you would sell to fund that, and then there would be smaller tranches of more junior paper. And the buyers of that paper, particularly the very senior paper, the triple-A paper, were not experts, they're not mortgage experts, they say, "It's triple-A? I'll buy it." This is conduit funds, accounts that are not set up to do hard-core analysis, they tend to just rely on the rating agencies. And again the spread that they're getting paid is very small, so they don't really have a lot of spread to play with to hire a lot of analysts to go and dig in the mortgage pools and really understand them, they kind of rely on the rating agencies, and that's their downfall. It's kind of an interesting interaction in the sense that a lot of this mortgage project was almost created by the bid for the CDO paper rather than the reverse. I mean, the traditional way to think about financing is, "Okay, I find an investment opportunity that on its face, I think, is a good opportunity. I want to deploy capital on that opportunity. Now I go look for funding. So I think that making mortgage loans is a good investment, so I will make mortgage loans. Then I will seek to fund those, to fund that activity, by issuing CDO paper, issuing the triple-A, double-A, A, and down the chain." But what happened is, you had the creation of so many vehicles designed to buy that paper, the triple-A, the double-A, all the CDO paper . . . that the dynamic flipped around. It was almost as if the demand for that paper created the mortgages.

**n+1:** Created the loans?

**HFM:** Called forth the loans, because it became a really profitable business. You saw where you could issue these liabilities. Say I could issue these liabilities at a weighted average cost of LIBOR [London Interbank Offered Rate] plus 150 [basis points], and I know all I have to do is just push that money out the door, push that money out the door, LIBOR plus 300, and I'll make a huge amount of money from doing that origination activity or just on the equity piece that I keep, which is highly, highly leveraged. The person who really knows the mortgages is not the person who is really taking most of the risk. The person who is taking most of the risk is the kind of undifferentiated mass of buyers out there.

**n+1:** Right, and when you say the person who knows the mortgage, meaning the person who knows that the person they find on the street . . .

**HFM:** May not be a good credit, right? What tends to happen in financial markets is, bad things happen when you really divorce the people who take the risk from the people who understand the risk. What happened is that that distance in the subprime market just increased and increased and increased. I mean, it started out that you had mortgage companies that would keep some of the stuff on their own books. Subprime lenders, it wasn't a big business, it was a small business, and it was specialty lenders, and they made risky loans, and they would keep a lot of it on their books.

But then these guys were like, "You know, there are hedge fund buyers for pools that we put together," and then the hedge fund buyers say, "You know what? We need to fund, we need to leverage this, so how can we leverage this? Oh, I have an idea, let's create a CDO and issue paper against it to fund ourselves," and then you get buyers of that paper. The buyers of that paper, they're more ratings-sensitive than fundamentals-sensitive, so they're quite divorced from the details. Then it got even more extended in the sense that vehicles were set up that had a mandate to kind of robotically buy that paper and fund themselves through issuing paper in the market.

**n+1:** Black boxes?

**HFM:** No, not the black boxes. But there wasn't a lot of human judgment going on. In reality those guys were so far from the true collateral that underlay the paper—they have no idea. It's like they're buying CP [commercial paper] of a conduit, the conduit's buying triple-A paper of a CDO, the CDO is set up by a hedge fund that's bought mortgage pools from a mortgage originator, and the mortgage originator is the one who realizes that they lent half a million dollars on a house in Stockton, California, to . . . someone who makes $50,000 a year. That's where the specific knowledge about the risk resides, but the ultimate risk taker is very, very far away from that.

So what happened is this machine, let's call it, a big machine that wanted to gobble up, you know, rated paper—needed to be fed. There were people who could make a lot of money feeding the machine, and they were like, "We need to keep originating mortgages, and feeding them to the machine," and if you have a robot bid, you tend to get a bubble. Someone is hungry for paper, paper will be created.

And that's almost never a good thing that lending decisions are being driven by the fact that many, many steps down the chain there's just someone who wants to buy paper.

**n+1:** Mmm-hmmm. But isn't—when you say that people started treating triple-A paper like money—isn't money also like money, in that sense?

**HFM:** Well, yeah, our money is fiat money, but a dollar is a dollar. You can use it to pay your tax liabilities, right? It's legal tender for all debts. If you have a debt, you can always use the dollar to pay off the debt.

**n+1:** You can't buy a coffee in London with a dollar.

**HFM:** Well, that's true, that's true. If your only use for money is buying coffees in London and you have dollars, then you have a problem.

+ + +

**n+1:** Why was all the press about the mortgage crisis about the hedge funds?

**HFM:** People like talking about hedge funds. They like to blame us for everything. And there were hedge funds that lost a lot of money.

**n+1:** That's why I offered to buy you a water.

**HFM:** Oh? We've had our share of lumps from the black boxes and subprime, but we're still standing.

**n+1:** You lost on the subprime?

**HFM:** We did. We were involved in creating CDOs.

**n+1:** You were?!

**HFM:** Yeah, yeah. Not me personally. But we have people who did it. They would buy mortgage pools, they would package them into CDOs, have an investment bank sell off the senior liabilities, and we kept the equity pieces ourselves, and, you know, those equity pieces are worth—they're worth pretty much zero, as far as I can tell. But the amount of money that was lost by us was only a portion of the amount that was lost on the whole on the dumb lending decisions that it turns out originators made. Okay, let's just say hypothetically we had the equity on a CDO with half a billion dollars in mortgage collateral, and we issued paper for $450 million and kept $50 million of the most junior piece for ourselves. Okay, so we lost $50 million. But if that mortgage pool is now only worth $300 million, it's $200 million of losses, $150 million in losses are borne by the people who bought the CDO paper.

**n+1:** From you?

**HFM:** Well, technically from an investment bank that managed the sale of paper from the CDO we set up.

**n+1:** So, from you?

**HFM:** When you buy a bottle of Coke from the A&P, did you buy it from the Coca-Cola Company or from A&P? If it turns out to be flat, you'd probably take it back to A&P, but you'd also maybe write an angry letter to the Coca-Cola Company. They bought something that in a sense we made, from a bank intermediary.

**n+1:** Are they mad at you?

**HFM:** Well, our CDO paper performed better than average. In comparison to the overall quality of mortgage origination in the last, call it, three or four years, ours was really much better. So I think they're happy we did a better job than our competitors—but they're not happy they lost money.

**n+1:** Is the person who ran that—is he going to get fired?

**HFM:** He was already fired.

**n+1:** Really? He's gone?

**HFM:** He's gone.

**n+1:** I should buy *him* a water.

**HFM:** You should buy him a water. But you know, there were other issues with him. It wasn't only that he lost money.

But to get back to the paradigm shifts, here was a guy who knows the market really, really well, who is a real expert in the nuts and bolts of mortgage lending, and really knew the collateral really well—but he was a true believer, and I think a lot of people were who were in that paradigm. "You know what, subprime is a really good thing, it's opening up home ownership to people who couldn't get it before for reasons that didn't really have to do with their ability to pay but had to do with outmoded criteria for thinking about credit." And "Most of these mortgages were going to pay off fine and the housing collateral behind them was solid."

And there were other people at the firm, say, at the middle of last year, who were not mortgage experts, who were saying, "I see the run-up in housing prices in some of these geographies, and I just don't really get it. I go down to Florida and see the forest of cranes, and I just wonder, who's going to be in all those apartments? And I hear about all sorts of friends who are getting loans to buy apartments or houses speculatively and who are lying about the fact that it's not a primary residence, and I see these commercials on TV, you know, about low-doc, no-doc mortgages—and there is no way, *there is no way* that this is not going to end badly. And I see that these mortgages are being created by this massive demand for CDO paper, by this robotic bid, and this is the perfect example of a bubble—and we should be short, we should be short subprime paper."

**n+1:** This is what guys do? They travel around Florida, they watch TV?

**HFM:** Just in your normal life. Like me—I trade a different market, I don't trade subprime, but I travel for other reasons, and some of my partners do the same thing. And we all, a number of us, thought, "This is just crazy. We should be short. This is a bubble waiting to be popped." But the person who was the expert, the person who ran the subprime business, who traded subprime paper and issued the CDOs, he was a true believer in the paradigm: "In 2003, people said that the credit quality of the average subprime mortgage was deteriorating, and now look, those mortgages have performed fine. The subprime market works."

And, hey, he was the expert—you defer to the expert.

**n+1:** He didn't listen.

**HFM:** But he's the expert, right? It's a tough thing. If you have somebody who's really trained in the mortgage business, he's been in the mortgage business for fifteen years, in equilibrium he'll do a great job. He'll be able to pick, of the mortgage pools out there, which is the good one, which is the bad one. He did a very good job of that, because the ones that he picked were better than the market. But in terms of detecting the paradigm shift, the guy who's just buried in the forest . . . he's not going to see the big picture, he's not going to catch the paradigm shift.

**n+1:** When he saw the cranes in Florida, when he saw the commercials on TV, what did he think?

**HFM:** I think his view was, the people who were predicting a crash in subprime were not experts in the subprime market. They were guys just basing their conclusions on anecdotal evidence. "But look, I'm knee deep in the data, I see the remittance reports every month, I've been involved in the 2003 subprime issuance and the 2004 subprime issuance, and people said that stuff was dodgy, but it's performed very well. And I know all the details. You have anecdotes? I have details."

And in equilibrium, yeah, if I tried to pick out of the mortgage pool which one is good and which one is bad based on having seen some cranes in Florida and hearing some stories about people taking out loans—

**n+1:** At a bar.

**HFM:** Yeah, I had a conversation at a bar, this guy told me he was making a ton of money flipping houses. You know, you're not going to become a mortgage trader based on that. But you might catch the paradigm shift. So this guy was really, you know, he was very much at the detail level, and missed the paradigm shift.

**n+1:** And now he's gone.

**HFM:** And now he will have plenty of time to think about the big picture.

**n+1:** [*laughs evil laugh*]

**HFM:** [*also laughs evil laugh*]

Six months pass. The damage from subprime mortgages turns out to be much worse than anyone expected. Throughout this period and the period to come, banks with serious exposure to mortgage-related assets engage in heated debates with investors and critics over the valuation of these assets. "Mark-to-market" means that companies are supposed to value their assets at their current market price when drawing up their profit-and-loss statements—but what if there is no market? Critics begin referring to companies overvaluing their assets as playing "mark-to-make-believe."

As 2007 turns into 2008, some indications of the size of the problem come into view. In October, after Merrill Lynch announces that it will be writing down more than $8 billion in subprime and other mortgage-related assets, its chief, Stan O'Neal, is forced out. In February, UBS, a large Swiss bank that is always being tricked into poor investments by slick American bankers, announces an enormous $11.3 billion fourth-quarter 2007 loss, due entirely to deterioration in U.S. mortgage-backed securities. A month later, Bear Stearns, one of the country's largest investment banks, which had taken the most serious initial hit from the subprime CDOs, enters a tailspin from which it won't recover. In a theme that will repeat over the coming months, erosion of confidence begets deterioration of credit. A brutal Wall Street Journal article, "Bear CEO's Handling of Crisis Raises Issues," documents the amount of time legendary Bear head Jimmy Cayne is spending out of town playing bridge and golf, "according," the Journal scrupulously notes, "to golf, bridge and hotel records." On Friday, March 14, 2008, after heavy client withdrawals, the bank stands on the brink of bankruptcy. Over the weekend it is saved, at a humiliatingly low price, by JPMorgan Chase.

For our second interview we met at HFM's fund in Manhattan.

# HFM II

# THE DEATH OF BEAR

March 26, 2008
Dow Jones Industrial Average: 12,422.86
Liquid Universe Corporate Index Spread over Benchmark: 231
U.S. OTR ten-year: 3.46 percent
Unemployment rate: 5.1 percent
Foreclosures: 223,651

**n+1:** So this is a hedge fund.

**HFM:** This is a hedge fund. Now you've seen what a hedge fund looks like: a lot of flat screens, a lot of people staring intently into them, and not a lot of noise. We're quite quiet for a hedge fund. We don't have TVs—that's one of the big differences probably between this trading floor and a typical trading floor is that I got rid of TVs some time ago. I don't have a TV at home, and I thought it was ironic that I had gone through all this effort to resist having a TV at home and then I would spend all day watching *Squawk Box* on CNBC, so then we decided we'll just get rid of the volume, we'll kill the volume, and then I spent my whole day inventing dialogue for Maria Bartiromo and new texts for the—well, there was this foot fungus commercial that would play on CNBC all the time, which was really disgusting, and we were coming up with new variations for the foot fungus ad. So we decided finally we really have to get rid of TVs. Other than that it's pretty standard.

**n+1:** This whole floor is your floor?

**HFM:** This is my floor, and we have one more floor underneath this.

**n+1:** This is your personal floor?

**HFM:** There are other people, I think you saw. But I'm fairly solipsistic.

**n+1:** So how are things going?

**HFM:** It's been a really turbulent couple of weeks. Obviously the market has been in some degree of crisis since the last time we spoke, but what's new is that it's really been spreading. I've been doing this for over a decade and I've seen asset prices generally more distressed than they are today—the equity market has been much more distressed than it is today. The particular market that I trade, I've seen prices much more distressed than they are today. But I've never seen the financial system as a whole more distressed. Banks, the sense of panic and despair at the major banks, I've just never seen it before.

So that's the background. We're operating in a world that's unknown.

**n+1:** When we talked a few months ago, you seemed okay with things; you thought everything was going fine, America was going to win this.

**HFM:** Well, I didn't want you to start a bank run with your vast readership at *n+1*. I felt it was my responsibility as a member of the financial community to keep all of literary New York from lining up at the bank or at the ATM the next day.

I still think things will be fine, but I overestimated the degree to which the subprime risk had been off-laid by the banks. I think a lot of it was off-laid—we talked about European buyers and Asian buyers who were the ultimate underwriters of the risk, but as it turns out, much more of the risk than I expected was still on the books of the big investment banks. So when you hear about write-downs related to subprime mortgages taking place at Merrill Lynch, Citibank, Bear Stearns, that's a consequence of their having retained risk related to these assets on their books. We thought it had been sold on to Europeans. And it was: The Germans lost a lot of money, and some of the Chinese banks are announcing earnings in the next weeks, and the speculation is that a lot of them will have to announce write-downs related to subprime. But Citibank had a ton of this stuff on their books and had to write down a tremendous amount. Almost all of the major banks have.*

At the end of the subprime orgy, it became difficult to place a lot of this debt. So the banks would end up warehousing it—they didn't know it was ten minutes to midnight. They had a profitable business in purchasing and securitizing these assets, but it was ten minutes to midnight and they didn't know it. They thought they would be able to place it and securitize it when things calmed down. But it turned out the clock struck midnight and these assets turned into—pumpkins. And they couldn't move them, and while all these assets were sitting on their books the real estate market started to deteriorate, and the value of these subprime mortgages started to deteriorate with it.

n+1: How long have they known?

---

* In the Global Financial Stability Report for the first half of 2009, the IMF estimated losses by U.K., European, and Asian banks on U.S. assets of $386 billion. In the same report, the estimate for U.S. banks is $966 billion.

**HFM:** The biggest write-downs mostly were taking place in the fourth quarter of '07, and they've continued. We've seen some more for the first quarter of 2008. There may be more to come, but for subprime the write-downs may be close to finished.* What people are worried about now and what's created a lot of tension in the financial markets is that the rot is spreading to other asset classes. So it's not just subprime mortgages: Now people say, "Gosh, subprime mortgages have performed so poorly that it's weighing on real estate markets, and that means that our Alt-A mortgages will perform poorly. That means people should be worried about prime mortgages, too. People should be worried about companies that are exposed to the consumer who is taking out a subprime mortgage or companies that relied on spending from consumers that was based on home equity—people withdrawing equity from their homes to buy things."

When you're talking about risk management, there's an assumption that not every asset class will be correlated. So, sure, subprime blows up, but the bank's okay because prime will hold up, or there won't be a perfect correlation with leveraged loans. But what's going on is that all these credit products are performing badly at once.

**n+1:** Because?

**HFM:** Because there are some real linkages. If consumer spending has been supported by people extracting equity from their homes, the mortgage market shutting down will hit consumer spending. And that will hurt companies that rely on consumer spending.

And then there are the financial linkages—hedge funds blowing up, so that they can't buy leveraged loans anymore, or banks that got hurt in subprime that have to sell down leveraged loans to generate liquidity, and the buyers are gone.

---

* Not by a long shot! According to the IMF, total U.S. bank write-downs from the end of the second quarter of 2007 to the end of the second quarter of 2008 amounted to $243 billion. By the end of the second quarter of 2009, write-downs had swollen to $610 billion.

So that's one financial linkage, but also there's capital—the banks' capital base. Every time a bank takes a write-down, that erodes its capital base, and the bigger the base the more risk it can take. There are rules for that—Basel II capital adequacy—and if a bank is writing down $10 billion, suddenly the risk-taking capability is reduced. Assume basically the capital adequacy ratio for all these banks is 10 percent. So if a bank falls $10 billion below its capital adequacy target, that's $100 billion in risk-taking capacity that disappears.

**n+1:** And this is regulated by the Fed?

**HFM:** Yes, among other regulators. The rules can be relaxed—there can be regulatory forbearance—but so far there hasn't been any and there probably shouldn't be because these rules are there for good reason. A good illustration of what can happen is Bear Stearns. Bear is not a commercial bank, it's an investment bank: It doesn't have these capital adequacy rules, it's not regulated by the Fed, and Bear, if your average bank had a capital adequacy rate supporting 10:1 leverage, Bear is more like 30:1. And that is one of the reasons confidence evaporated so quickly: People looked at the balance sheet and realized that if assets have to be written down even a small amount, Bear can be insolvent. And that creates a panic

In reality I don't think they had a solvency issue, but when the capital cushion is so small it creates instability.*

+ + +

---

\* Whether Bear was solvent still elicits debate. One interesting piece of evidence is the fate of Maiden Lane LLC. This is the vehicle through which the Fed, to support JPMorgan Chase's purchase of Bear Stearns, underwrote just under $29 billion of difficult-to-price securities owned by Bear. As of June 30, 2009, the Fed reported that the fair value of the Maiden Lane portfolio had declined to just over $26 billion. Not a great performance, but not so bad that it suggests Bear was insolvent.

**n+1:** Can you tell me what happened with Bear Stearns? What were the steps?

**HFM:** Bear was a bank that was very involved in the asset-backed and subprime market, both as a principal and as an agent.

What happened this summer was funds managed by Bear Stearns—not things on their own books, other people's funds that they manage, other people's capital—those funds were heavily leveraged and invested in asset-backed securities. Those funds blew up—they went into uncontrolled combustion. They failed very quickly. One day they were there, the next all the assets were marked down, then they were insolvent and folded up. Now, that's not Bear Stearns's capital, but there were guys sitting in the Bear Stearns office.

**n+1:** Which is where?

**HFM:** On 47th and Madison. Just down the street.

**n+1:** And they were sitting there; they had a little hedge fund—

**HFM:** Which means they raised money from outside investors—they get paid based on how the fund does, they get a percentage of the profits. And they traded in subprime assets where the capital was given to them by outside investors.

They were sitting there, buying asset-backed securities backed by subprime mortgages, they were borrowing a lot of money, they used the capital they had, they borrowed outside money, they bought subprime mortgages. They were highly, highly leveraged, 50:1 leverage.*

---

* Ralph Cioffi and Matthew Tannin, the top managers of the Bear Stearns High Grade Structured Credit Strategies fund and the Bear Stearns High Grade Structured Enhanced fund, were indicted in June 2008 for allegedly misrepresenting the condition of the funds to investors.

**n+1:** Why was Bear Stearns in particular doing this?

**HFM:** Bear Stearns supposedly had an expertise in subprime and asset-backed securities; it is an expertise of theirs. They're still alive.

**n+1:** Really?

**HFM:** You know when somebody falls off a motorcycle and they want to harvest their organs, they're still alive until they harvest the organs. Right now Bear Stearns, there's an EKG, it is pinging, they're technically still alive and JPMorgan is waiting for the health care proxy to sign and say they can start harvesting the organs. This is where Bear is right now. They had an expertise.

**n+1:** So it was $100 billion? How much money?

**HFM:** I don't know. It was not huge, $1 to $2 billion each. In that range. Which doesn't make them huge funds. Modest funds.

But from that moment forth, people on the market speculated as to how many similar kinds of assets Bear Stearns must own on its own books. There was a cloud of suspicion over Bear Stearns. As it turns out, I don't know that they were in that much trouble. They were probably much more careful with their own money than outside money, but once there's a cloud of suspicion, the information asymmetry that exists between people outside the firm, who don't know what's going on, and inside the firm can create a crisis of confidence.

**n+1:** Can't the firm say, "Look, we have this, we have that . . ."?

**HFM:** What are they going to do? Are they going to show you every instrument they have on their books? People don't know what these instruments are. Like an asset-backed bond—what's it worth? Nobody knows what it's worth; there isn't a market for this anymore.

It's not like there are three bond issues and that's it; there are thousands, and each one is backed by thousands of mortgages. It just becomes an information-processing problem. You simply can't prove to me in a reasonable amount of time that everything's fine.

**n+1:** They don't have other instruments besides mortgages?

**HFM:** They do, they have their building, that's one of the things that is probably worth the most. But Bear was involved in a lot of the asset classes that had problems. First it's subprime mortgages, then it's leveraged loans—they're exposed to all these things, thirty times leveraged, so a very small diminution of the value of these assets could mean that their equity is worth nothing. And it's just going to be impossible for these guys to prove to everyone's satisfaction in a short period of time with a high degree of precision that their assets are worth what they say they're worth. There's been a cloud over Bear Stearns for eight months, and in retrospect people were critical of their management for being insufficiently aggressive in trying to persuade people that everything was fine. They simply asserted that everything was fine.

**n+1:** Did they come here, have lunch?

**HFM:** No, we're not a big customer, but they did speak to other customers and they did speak in the press, and they came off as a bit cavalier. And as the credit environment deteriorated, the nervousness about them and the rumors about them intensified, and it culminated in a process where a lot of customers who had money at Bear Stearns, customers of their prime brokerage business and regular retail investors, said, "I don't want my money there. Why not move it to Citi or Goldman to be safe?" And once that process starts, as each account withdraws, it becomes even more enticing for the other guy to withdraw because it looks like things are unwinding. And then institutional counterparties start to refuse to take Bear's credit . . .

**n+1:** Are they an investment broker? If you had to take your money, you had to call up your buddy?

**HFM:** Yeah, and the broker could try to persuade you. And look, "I could be wrong about Bear being in trouble and I could lose a little money moving it around and so on and impose upon myself the inconvenience of moving my money—a little money and a little brain damage. But if I'm wrong and leave it, I could lose a lot of money." That's the balance of risk.

**n+1:** It'll cause you brain damage?

**HFM:** Not literal brain damage but, you know, inconvenience—brain damage. So on one hand you're going to impose an inconvenience on yourself, but on the other—it unwound very quickly. On Thursday they said everything was fine, on Friday they had withdrawals of a magnitude that they had to go to the Fed. They're not regulated by the Fed, so it's unusual for the Fed to be lending money to Bear Stearns, but an agreement was put in place to try to provide the liquidity to Bear Stearns, and over the weekend a deal was struck for JPMorgan to help.

**n+1:** The government struck that deal?

**HFM:** The government had their role. The difference between what happened and a normal takeover is the Fed, because the Fed is providing JPMorgan some non-recourse financing for Bear Stearns assets. The strange thing about the deal is that Morgan is paying so little for Bear Stearns. Bear Stearns was trading at $170 a share not that long ago; now the deal was $2 a share. A lot of wealth was wiped out. The question is, why would anyone accept it? Just before you came in today, JPMorgan increased their offer to $10. But a $2 share offer, for the most part it's "This is like pennies to me. I'll say no to this deal and maybe I'll do better in bankruptcy." The reason the Fed didn't want Bear to go through bankruptcy is that there are all kinds of interconnections between Bear and other banks. There's counterparty risk, it could lead to panic, it could lead to a whole mess in the financial market, so the Fed just wants the problem to go away, the Treasury just wants the problem to go away. But if I am a shareholder, it's not my problem. "Let's go bankrupt, let's see, maybe we can do better than $2!" So everyone here was puzzled that Bear would agree to that kind of a deal.

Now, Bear Stearns is unusual in that a lot of the shares are owned by insiders in the company, and the theory we had at the desk here is that the Treasury Department—not the Fed, the Fed's not so tough, but the Treasury Department—went to the top guys at Bear and said: "Either a deal gets done that saves Bear and calms the financial system by the end of this weekend, or we will find some reason to put you in jail." And I think one of the things that every officer of a public company is very sensitive to, post-Enron, is jail. There has been a criminalization of failure. And after Sarbanes-Oxley, and in the wake of prosecutions related to business failures, it was like Beria said: "You show me the man, I'll find the crime."

So I think for these guys it wasn't just "I'm risking $2 if I say no," it was "I'm risking $2 plus anal rape in jail."

**n+1:** I don't think they put them in that kind of jail.

**HFM:** Okay, then tennis. "I'm risking exposing the weaknesses of my tennis game." So anyway, that was the reason that deal was struck.

**n+1:** And the Treasury, those guys are tough?

**HFM:** Well, Hank Paulson is tough, yeah.

It was very strange because the Fed providing liquidity to Bear Stearns is kind of unprecedented. It's not regulated by the Fed, and if it turns out that the Fed finds that an institution like Bear Stearns is so integral to the smooth functioning of the financial system that it needs to bail it out, it makes you wonder whether the regulatory regime has to be pretty radically overhauled.

**n+1:** And the Fed has more money than anyone?

**HFM:** The Fed can print money. They can create money. They can't create value but they can create money. To the extent that there are dollar claims that people have on banks and the banks can't satisfy those claims, the banks can take assets they have to the Fed and borrow dollars against those assets.

**n+1:** The Fed can print money over the weekend.

**HFM:** No, it's not quantitative easing, but in this case they lent Treasuries—assets that people will treat just like money—against risky assets that Bear had on its books. That's why they're the lender of last resort, because they have as many dollars as they need to lend. In this case they used Treasury bonds from their portfolio. But if they go and print money promiscuously, the dollar won't be worth very much.

**n+1:** [*glumly*] It's already not.

**HFM:** And one of the reasons the dollar is doing so poorly is that there are worries about our financial system and people anticipate that the Fed will have to run an easier monetary policy in order to deal with it.

**n+1:** What's going to happen to the guys who worked at Bear Stearns?

**HFM:** Some of them will wind up working for Morgan and a lot will be laid off, and people talk about it as a bailout but I don't think it's a bailout of Bear's management or shareholders. The shareholders get maybe $10 a share, but they used to trade at $170 per share, so they're pretty much wiped out. The senior management is all gone. And some people say a quarter, some people say half will be laid off.

If you really look at what the Treasury and/or the Fed was doing, they know they have to protect the financial system from grinding to a halt, but they don't want to create a moral hazard as a result of people thinking they're going to get bailed out no matter what. So yes, there was a bailout of the counterparties, but they needed to take Bear out and shoot it in front of everybody. So they took it out. At a $2 offer, all the senior management is gone, and that's the financial equivalent of taking the shareholders out and shooting them.

From time to time you have to kill a management team to encourage the others. So now Citibank and Merrill Lynch realize that it's unlikely that they'll be allowed to default. But at the same time the people who are actually taking risk, the senior managers at Merrill Lynch, know if a blowup happens, regardless of the fact that the institutions may be saved, their shareholdings will be worth zero, and their job tenure will be done.

**n+1:** Wouldn't it have been better to let them go bankrupt?

**HFM:** And let their counterparties face the music? Maybe, but the parlous condition of the financial system as a whole, I think, persuaded the Fed that this is not the time to experiment and see how interconnected the system has become.

If we were in a calm economic environment and Bear, for non-systemic reasons, failed—say they put all their money into Cheese-Sandwich.com, and they failed for that reason—then it might be appropriate to let them go bankrupt because the rest of the financial system would be stable. Even if it inflicts losses on the rest of the financial system and causes a lot of brain damage for me, it won't be a risk to the system as a whole.

But every bank out there to some degree or another is suffering the same problems that led to the cloud of suspicion over Bear. So this is not a great time to test a proposition that the financial system can cope with disorderly unwinding of all these contracts.

**n+1:** Why is it that after eight months of suspicion this happened in forty-eight hours?

**HFM:** That's one of these crazy things about bank runs, it's not clear what triggers them. I was actually in Argentina the day of the bank run in 2000, and I couldn't tell you why it happened that day. It was beautiful weather, I was having meetings—

**n+1:** Steaks?

**HFM:** No, meetings, this was too early, during banking hours, and I was running around having meetings that were taking place in an office building of a bank called Banco General de Negocios. And everything was great and then when I came down the elevator at the end of the day, late afternoon, there was a line of people out the door of the bank, and I can't tell you why it was that day. Argentina had been in economic difficulty for the prior year, but that day the bank run started. And then they had to impose basically a deposit freeze.

**n+1:** Were people mad?

**HFM:** That's what started the unraveling of the Argentine government; people were standing outside banks banging on pots and pans. The run started the day I was there.

**n+1:** Did you run from the run?

**HFM:** There was a big line and I went to the airport.

**n+1:** And you were here the Thursday that the Bear Stearns run happened.

**HFM:** We were just sitting here watching. It was amazing how the stock just dove. It had been trading poorly for months, but it lost 60 percent of its value in a couple of hours. And we were mesmerized just watching on our Reuters screens. And everyone in the market was doing the same thing—the phone stopped ringing, I stopped getting Bloomberg messages, everyone was just watching: "It can't be! What's going on? Stuff doesn't lose that much value on no news in a couple of hours."

And really what was going on was that there was a run going on against Bear and people were getting wind of it.

**n+1:** There was no news, Bear never announced—

**HFM:** Nothing like that. In fact, they were going to come out and say everything was fine. I don't want to pick on Bear, but it was just incredible. And then what happened in subsequent days is that similar prophecies—stock price prophecies—happened to other financial stocks, and rumormongers thought they could spread rumors and drive down the stock of other financial companies. Or maybe everybody just came to the same conclusions themselves. The same thing happened to Lehman, but they were able to restore confidence and the stock went back up.*

**n+1:** How?

**HFM:** I think their liquidity situation was much stronger than Bear's, and most importantly, people saw that the Fed and the Treasury had

---

* Not for long! Lehman stock went from just under 46 on March 14 to as low as 20.25 on the 15th before rebounding to 46 again on the 16th. From the beginning of May it never saw such levels again.

arranged some sort of bailout for Bear's counterparties, that they were trying to firewall the problem, and that a completely disorderly outcome for Lehman, even if Lehman was in similar shape to Bear, was unlikely. I think also part of it had to do with the management of Lehman, which had been much more convincing about why Lehman was in solid shape, not just the day the stock share started to fall but in the months running up to that.

**n+1:** Can you talk about what the hedge fund might have done to make money?

**HFM:** We could have been trading the debt of Bear Stearns, which gyrated wildly. There are credit default swaps, which are an instrument where you trade credit risk of a borrower. One-year credit default swaps on Bear Stearns at their height were trading at 2,000 basis points, or 20 percent—you would have to pay 20 percent a year to ensure yourself against the default of Bear Stearns, and today it's about 200. They went from 200 to 2,000 to 200 in the space of a week. We could have traded that, but we were staring in awe instead of making money! We didn't lose any money, either, so I guess we got entertainment out of it, which has some value. Now, we could have made money to buy entertainment; instead we just watched screens and got entertainment directly and that's not taxed!

+ + +

**n+1:** Is this your actual office? It's so small.

**HFM:** Yes. I don't actually spend much time in here, I have a desk out on the trading floor, so this is just for meetings or phone calls I can't take out of the desk, or interviews with literary magazines that I do every Wednesday at 4 p.m.

**n+1:** So there's a financial meltdown. Are you worried?

**HFM:** Worried about what specifically? I am always worried. I'm not worried about a catastrophic unwind at this point. Our fund is extremely conservative, we have a ton of liquidity, and we've always run our business to be robust in financial crises. We're not directional and we're not highly leveraged. The downside is that in good times we've generated solid returns but we're never, you know, up 80 percent or 100 percent. It's a low-risk fund by design.

**n+1:** What about when you lost $50 million in subprime?

**HFM:** I told you that? I never said a number! We're not going to talk about that. But that is about as much money as we're ever going to lose, and we had planned that that was the amount of risk we would take to that asset class and our worst possible outcome for that asset class happened. I don't want to get into too much detail, but we weren't in the situation where our lenders were pulling lines to us or we couldn't cope with investor withdrawals. We were at a low degree of leverage, so I'm not worried about that.

I do worry about the hedge fund business—I think that it may wind up being a much more difficult business going forward for various reasons. You've had a number of fund blowups in the past couple of months. These are all pretty high-profile funds that either endured very large losses which put into jeopardy the existence of the fund or blew it up completely. I think that damages the credibility of the asset class. People who invest in hedge funds have thought of it as an asset class that would be robust in any environment, that you're getting the best investment talent, and you're least likely to have these kinds of disasters. But I think the outcomes of some of these funds give the lie to that belief. So what may happen is that even if we perform better than the average hedge fund—if everyone is down 10 percent and you're up 1 percent—you may have outperformed everybody, but the structural damage made to the asset class is so large that it doesn't matter that you outperformed, money is going to be pulled out of hedge funds.*

**n+1:** A hedge fund is an asset class?

**HFM:** I think we can talk about alternative investments—hedge funds and private equity—as an asset class.

**n+1:** Are hedge funds considered more aggressive?

**HFM:** The reason it's called a hedge fund is that originally the investment would be hedged to broad market factors. Now, it's a very plastic definition—just a leveraged investment vehicle—but I think people like to think of it as you're getting the best investment talent, the best risk management, because you're paying a lot more than you would pay for a mutual fund. And if hedge funds have a high probability of spectacular blowup, that makes it a less attractive asset class.

Number two is that people invest in funds-of-funds—vehicles that farm out money to several hedge funds on the theory that each one has its own investment strategy and their returns won't be correlated—but what we're seeing this year is a high degree of correlation of hedge fund assets. So if I was thinking I'd benefit my diversification by investing in multiple hedge funds but I'm not—in fact there's a hedge fund factor that underlies the performance of all these funds, so in bad times they can be much more correlated than I thought—then money might leave the asset class and this hurts everybody.

**n+1:** When you say you're paying fees, is it just a higher threshold?

**HFM:** The investors pay pretty rich fees to invest in a hedge fund.

---

* There is no one gold standard for hedge fund statistics, but according to BarclayHedge, hedge fund industry assets under management peaked at the end of 2007 at $2.1 trillion and by the second quarter of 2009 had dropped to under $1 trillion.

Often it's 2 percent per year and 20 percent of the profits—which is why it's great to be an HFM.

But to justify those fees you have to give people something they can't get from lower-cost investment vehicles. What hedge funds claimed to be providing was returns that weren't correlated to major market indices, returns that were superior to what you could get in other asset classes, and that you're getting the best talent and risk management and superior returns with lower risks. What we're seeing this year is that it's becoming a very risky asset class very quickly, and that it became an asset class with a high degree of correlation among funds.

**n+1:** What about the whole thing?

**HFM:** The financial system as a whole will be all right; the Fed and the Treasury did draw a line at Bear Stearns and the line held. We haven't seen any evidence of the average Joe going to a bank and pulling money out of his checking account. Terrible scenario number one, where the average person loses confidence and the banking system goes bankrupt like in Argentina—the probability of that in the U.S. is close to zero.

**n+1:** Doesn't everyone also owe credit card debt? They would show up at their bank and ask for their money, and the bank would say, "We want *our* money!"

**HFM:** I think people may owe their money to bank X and deposit it in bank Y, so it's not actually something they can set off against you. I think another bad path is the Japan scenario—where losses don't get recognized and all these banks are in worse shape than they let on, they don't take risks because they don't really have the capital, but they can't raise capital because they don't recognize the losses, so no one is going to invest in the bank if it hasn't given a true picture of its balance sheet. Then you have a sort of moribund system of zombie banks like in Japan, and that retards recovery, and you have an economy that can never build momentum to grow again.

**n+1:** They have zombie banks?

**HFM:** People talk about the banks in Japan post the crash of the early nineties as zombie companies and zombie banks—the bank has a loan to a company that is clearly insolvent, the bank should be doing a restructuring, but the bank doesn't want to admit the company is insolvent, so it doesn't restructure the loan, it's in limbo—they're, like, undead.

Today, where people have made bad investment decisions, where people built houses they never should have built, there's a misallocation of resources. The loss has already happened. The loss isn't what happens on a balance sheet; the loss is what happens when someone cuts down a tree, makes cement, builds a 6,000-square-foot house in a place it should never be built. So the loss has already happened. The question is, how do you allocate that loss? And if you don't allocate the loss, if you pretend it isn't there, then this has really baleful consequences for the economy. So what we're going through now is this process of loss allocation. It can be done swiftly, fairly, and intelligently, or it can be done slowly, and messily, and inefficiently, and also it can be not done at all. If it's happened, the best is to deal with it swiftly and fairly. And when the shareholders get hurt really badly and the banks have to recapitalize at punitive levels, or get taken over $2 a share, I think it's fair—the banks made bad decisions, the equity holders are the prime beneficiaries of the activities the bank is undertaking. When things go poorly, they should be the primary bearers of the loss. I think that's good.

**n+1:** They're not going to want to do that.

**HFM:** They're being forced to do that. The regulations are forcing them to do that and it's happening. I mean, Citigroup, Merrill Lynch raised capital, they did it at prices that I don't think they're happy about.

**n+1:** Their share prices went down.

**HFM:** They went down and they raised capital at that lower price. I think it's fair that those guys should bear the loss. Now, who else can take loss? Foolish borrowers—they lose their homes or wind up having to sell assets in order to pay back their debts. Or taxpayers can take the loss, through paying for some kind of bailout or through inflation, which isn't fair, but which is likely to happen to a certain degree. What's important is that this is done quickly and that when it's done there's certainty that loss has been recognized and that losses have been distributed, and then we can start moving again.

**n+1:** Otherwise we have zombies?

**HFM:** Otherwise we have these zombie banks that can't lend, zombie companies that shouldn't exist, and resources that should be released aren't being released.

I was just in Florida visiting family and it was amazing to see all the new housing that had been built that's just empty. I was visiting some relatives in a relatively upscale property development in south Florida that is twenty-five hundred homes and the initial phase sold out quickly, and many people who lived there decided to invest in the last phase of development and buy some units in order to resell them—and it's like it's a movie set or something. It's like a neutron bomb went off. There's no one there.

+ + +

**n+1:** What's the mood in the fund community?

HFM: In this fund? The mood is pretty good, but we really—I'll speak for myself—I really make a strong effort to be even-tempered on the trade floor because the enemy of intelligent trading is emotion. If you're crazy with fear or with greed you're going to make bad decisions, and emotion is a communicable disease, so you have to be calm. So the mood here is very calm.

n+1: If you allowed yourselves to be ruled by your emotions, what would you be?

HFM: I am by nature a nervous person, so I would be nervous. Not because of anything specific that's going on here or because it's going to collapse, but because we are going to go through a painful six to eighteen months of very slow or zero economic growth for the economy as a whole, which is never fun to live through, and second, there could be some real structural damage done to the hedge fund industry.

n+1: *Now* is America finished?

HFM: America is not finished. The fact that we've been able to confront these problems so quickly is exactly why I am in the long run optimistic about America's economy.

n+1: Though Bear Stearns spent eight months saying things were fine.

HFM: But in Japan it took ten years for some banks, ten years to come to grips with some of the problems that really originated in the crash of the late eighties or early nineties. When Russia defaulted on its ruble debt in '98, we knew of a Japanese company that had bought a lot of it. And we noticed that they never publicly disclosed the loss. Not just us; other people knew too. And somebody asked the management, "Didn't you own some hundreds of millions of dollars of GKO?" "Yes." "So aren't you going to take a loss?" "No . . . we plan on holding the debt to maturity." It was defaulted! That's failure to confront the problem.

**n+1:** Are there people now in American banks who know about losses and are trying to hide them?

**HFM:** I think the banks are doing their best to come up with an honest accounting of what their troubled assets really are worth. People's minds are boggled by the kinds of numbers we see every quarter when banks announce their write-downs, but we all know banks' losses are there. Everyone knows $2 trillion in subprime mortgages are out there and that one-quarter will go bad, so you can do the math and calculate the losses.* What would worry me is if I knew the losses were there but didn't see huge write-downs. Now, I didn't know whether the write-downs would be at U.S. banks or at German banks, but the losses had to be somewhere, and the fact that we're seeing them being recognized tells me the problem's being dealt with.

**n+1:** So you look out here onto midtown on the twentieth floor. This is all going to be okay?

**HFM:** That guy there will lose his job. White shirt, futzing about—he'll lose his job. He's putting. There's going to be no room for people like that, the bar is higher. You can't play golf in your office during a crisis.

**n+1:** Really?

**HFM:** I think he's holding a piece of paper, actually. That guy's done! Everyone else is okay.

---

* According to the Mortgage Bankers' Association National Delinquency Survey released in August 2009, the subprime delinquency rate is 25.25 percent.

In the spring and summer of 2008, things go from bad to worse, though the national news cycle is dominated by the dramatic electoral campaign of Barack Obama. In June and July the major banks announce large second-quarter losses: Merrill Lynch, $4.6 billion; Lehman, $2.87 billion; Citigroup, $2.5 billion. Shares of Fannie Mae and Freddie Mac, the giant semi-government mortgage holders, begin to tumble, with one former Federal Reserve governor saying, "Congress ought to recognize that these firms are insolvent." Markets grumble but at least think that this is as bad as it's going to get. By the end of the year the losses will mount into the tens of billions. Of the investment banks, Lehman appears to be the most troubled, and in June an executive coup brings a new management team to the top—too late. In July a large California commercial bank, IndyMac, is closed down by the FDIC due to the amount of bad low-doc mortgage loans on its books. Rumors begin to circulate that the Treasury will soon be forced to arrange a rescue of Fannie Mae and Freddie Mac.

After several years of unchecked growth, hedge fund assets peak and the fund industry as a whole begins to suffer from investors' withdrawals. Signs of stress become obvious in assets far away from the epicenter of the subprime crisis. In mid-July crude oil prices peak and begin a sharp descent. At the beginning of August several "hot" emerging-market currencies that had attracted tremendous investor interest rapidly cool off: The Russian ruble, Brazilian real, and Mexican peso all hit recent valuation highs and then rapidly depreciate.

# HFM III

## ON THE EVE

*September 4, 2008*
Dow: 11,188.23
Liquid Universe Corporate Index Spread over Benchmark: 263
U.S. OTR ten-year: 3.81 percent
Unemployment: 6.2 percent
Foreclosures: 303,879

**n+1:** We're back in your office above midtown. Last time we looked out, people were being fired, people were jumping out of windows.

**HFM:** And it's . . . continued largely in that vein. The credit crisis that was under way is still under way, and the recognition of losses that was sort of beginning is continuing—but it's still continuing at a pace that means that the situation is not resolved. We haven't reached the bottom. We haven't reached a point where people feel like all the bad news is out of the way. It's like a rainstorm of shoes: the shoes keep dropping, and there's still clouds in the sky, and there's still going to be more shoes dropping, and until the footwear stops falling, you know, the crisis will continue.

**n+1:** You were optimistic that companies were announcing their losses, were dealing with the bad news. Was that not correct?

**HFM:** No, they are, but people's estimates of the size of those losses have increased. If you talk about subprime, most of those losses have been recognized. But the losses extend beyond subprime, they extend beyond leveraged loans. So now people are worried about prime mortgages, now they're worried about development loans, mortgages of commercial property, so the losses have not really been recognized, or the loss recognition process there is only just beginning. Then you have the whole issue of Fannie Mae and Freddie Mac. If you look at Fannie and Freddie, the equity is *definitely* wiped out, these things are insolvent, the equity has been burned through—you have negative equity.* You have to recognize that. If you marked all their assets to market and said, "What are the assets worth?" and you compared them to the liabilities, you'd find that the assets are worth *less* than their liabilities, which means that the equity is worth nothing. If that were a regular company, and not a company that plays this really important infrastructural role in the mortgage market, they'd go bankrupt. This company goes bankrupt. The equity should be wiped out, and maybe some of the debt should be wiped out, and it needs to be restructured. But instead it's like the zombies, they're zombie companies, and because these companies are very politically powerful and also because they're important and there's fear that if they were to fail or if the equity holders were to be wiped out, that it would lead to a horrible shock in confidence. But I think that in the end—if you have a dead body in the room and I keep saying, "That person's not dead, that person's just resting," and pretty soon it starts to smell and decompose—there's only so long we can pretend before the odor becomes overpowering and we have to run from the room.

---

* Three days after the interview, both Fannie Mae and Freddie Mac were placed into conservatorship by their regulator, the Federal Housing Finance Agency.

**n+1:** And when we talked about the question of whether this was going to spread beyond the credit market, that seems to be happening?

**HFM:** Well, there are two kind of linkages we can talk about. One is the financial linkages. So does it spread to other categories of financial asset classes? And it has been—there's a problem in subprime, and then it moved to Alt-A, and now people are worried about prime and commercial mortgages. So there definitely has been a financial spreading. The other linkage you worry about is, "Do the problems in the financial system spread to the real economy?" To a certain extent, *obviously*, right? The financial system is a way of accounting for what's going on in the real economy. And so we see foreclosures, and unemployment ticking up, and job loss, but I think people have been actually surprised at the extent to which the real economy has been stable in the face of all this. I mean, technically we don't even have a recession yet! We haven't had negative GDP growth!* And that's kind of a mystery. I think that's another thing for people in the financial community, who say, "Gosh, things are so bad, pretty soon it's got to spread to the real economy." At a certain point if that recession never comes, then people will convince themselves that it's not going to come. But right now, the fact that it hasn't happened yet has not really changed anybody's assessment in the financial world that that damage is still coming.

**n+1:** And is it just that people are still maxing out their credit cards?

**HFM:** No, but one of the things that has been very beneficial for statistics in the U.S. has been exports. Exports have been a real bright spot because the dollar has been weak and the rest of the world has

---

* Not exactly. Subsequent to the interview, on December 1, 2008, the National Bureau of Economic Research Business Cycle Dating Committee declared that "a peak in economic activity occurred in the U.S. economy in December 2007. The peak marks the end of the expansion that began in November 2001 and the beginning of a recession." That said, the first quarter for which a really dramatic drop in GDP was reported was the third quarter of 2008.

been strong. The rest of the world is continuing to grow. People have talked about China being a very large source of growth, or some of the countries that have done well with high commodity prices, so Brazil, Russia, India, China. And growth has held up pretty well in these countries, and so that's been supportive to the real economy in the U.S. That may be changing, from what we are seeing—the emerging markets are starting to slow down and running into some more problems. And Europe, too, Europe is obviously more important to the emerging market in terms of economic weight, and Europe really seems to be going down.\* It's interesting—if you look at what's happening to the euro versus the dollar, it tells you that people are concerned about growth in Europe.

**n+1:** The euro is weakening?

**HFM:** The euro is weakening. The last time we talked everyone was talking about the dollar: "The dollar is going to get killed, it's going to be the end of the dollar." And I think I said, you know, it's very hard to project the future of the currency based on its recent past. The currency market tends to be ahead of events; it's a very forward-looking market. And so the dollar—in spite of all the prophecies—the dollar's been on a tear in the last couple of weeks, even the last two or three months, the dollar's been on a tear. That is because currency traders look at the rest of the world and they say, "What the U.S. is going through, the rest of the world is going to start to be affected by that." The rest of the world is slowing down, and therefore the currency market is saying, "All right, well, the rate cut to the U.S. may be a reach on their end, but you know they're actually just beginning in the rest of the world." Suddenly it's not so attractive to short the dollar along with everything else. I think we had this year of people

---

\* The European Union followed close behind the United States in slipping into recession. In March 2009, the Euro Area Business Cycle Dating Committee declared that economic activity peaked in January 2008.

very robotically selling dollars and buying every other currency in the world—first out of a sense of optimism about the emerging markets, you know, "I just want to be in the emerging market. There's so much growth potential there; I want to be exposed to the currency," then out of pessimism about the U.S.: "The financial situation in the U.S. is so terrible, the banks are in such rotten shape, I want to be out of dollars." So there's been a huge flow out of dollars. The world is short the dollar. Now suddenly people look at the world and they're just panicked, and they want to reduce risk. They just want to get back to flat, right? "I don't want to have any positions at all. I'm too scared," you know, "I just want to curl up into a ball."

**n+1:** And so if these other markets are slowing down, is their slowdown going to slow us down here?

**HFM:** It will probably have an impact on exports in the U.S. And this is of course the nightmare scenario, that the whole world slows down simultaneously and you get into a vicious circle.

**n+1:** And then what?

**HFM:** And then you have the Great Depression! I don't think that is going to happen. But the nightmare is that basically there's no source of growth anywhere in the world, you just basically have a shrinking of demand, a spreading wave of risk aversion all over the world, and you get into a liquidity trap. That's still a very extreme scenario.

**n+1:** When does this begin to feel like less of a cyclical thing, like the weather, and more of a permanent end-of-the-world kind of thing?

**HFM:** When you see me selling apples out on the street, that's when you should go stock up on guns and ammunition.

It's interesting because it gets to the issue of: How should policy react to what's going on? And you can tend to break people into two camps. There are people who say, "There needs to be robust government intervention. The government needs to prop up asset prices in order to keep banks solvent. There needs to be a buyer of last resort, and that buyer of last resort is going to be the only player with the balance sheet to do it: It's going to be the government, it's going to be the U.S. government, the Treasury." And then there are people who say, "No. Really what needs to happen is that we need to finish this process of loss recognition, the faster the better, so that there's full transparency as to the true financial condition of banks—of companies, of Fannie and Freddie, of everybody—and then prices [of financial assets] get marked to levels that reflect their true condition and that don't have embedded in them the expectation, this entrenched expectation, of continued decline." There's some price at which the consumer knows it's a bargain: Everything's just been marked down.

And which camp you fall into isn't just a matter of ideology; it's a matter of how bad you think the problem really is. Because if you had a factory, and you're like, "The factory is having problems," one of the ways of recognizing loss is you could say to the equity holders, "Sorry, the equity holders' claim is worth nothing; it really now belongs to the debt holder." What you're doing is you're shuffling claims—you're not doing anything to the factory, you're shuffling claims. And once you're done shuffling those claims so the right people own it and everybody knows the financial condition, the factory can continue producing.

What it could be, though, instead you just go in and you just like smash all the equipment in the factory. Right? Then you've done real damage, right? The factory just doesn't work anymore.

And when you talk about financial institutions, if you say we can mark everything down to its true condition, you're saying the mark-downs themselves don't cause damage to the institution. The institution is still there, the bank is still there. There's still people that show up to work; you haven't lost all the intellectual capital. These banks continue to exist.

But there's some people who think the problem is so bad that if you actually recognize the losses, that it's akin to smashing the equipment in the factory. Because these institutions can't exist anymore, right? That for a bank, if you say, "Look, you can't exist anymore. You're so deeply insolvent that everybody's fired and everybody's got to leave," at that point financial intermediation won't work anymore. It doesn't matter that you've marked everything down to the level that makes sense—*you don't have a financial system anymore.* And a lot of people think that's one of the reasons the Great Depression was so difficult to get out of, that the financial machinery was smashed. So I think which camp you fall into depends a little on how bad you think the damage is.

Personally, I don't think the losses are so large that if you recognized them it would be the end of the financial system. Some people would suffer pretty seriously—if you owned shares at certain banks, if you owned shares at Fannie or Freddie. Right now what we're doing, trying to recognize the loss in a slower fashion, or talking about policy solutions where that loss would be effectively apportioned out to people in a stealthy manner by inflation or by fiscalization—that is delaying the loss recognition process and creating an entrenched expectation that prices of financial assets are going to continue to go down. And it's interesting, people continue to say, "What's happening? There's no money." Well, there's plenty of money. I saw an interesting article today about the cash holdings of hedge funds, that hedge funds are sitting on $600 billion *of cash.* So it's not a question of lack of cash. It's a question of lack of risk taking; it's a lack of risk appetite. And the reason there's no risk appetite is because every day I come in, gas prices are higher; every day I come in, credit spreads are wider; every day I come in, there's some other piece of bad news that's being disclosed. Why should I take risk?

**n+1:** The hedge funds are keeping cash under the mattress?

**HFM:** A lot of cash. Part of it is we don't feel we have transparency into how bad the losses are. And we also worry, ourselves, about whether our investors are going to want their money back, so we're sitting on our cash.

**n+1:** They can just show up one day and ask for their money back?

**HFM:** No, there are limits on how much they can withdraw, to preserve the stability of the fund, and most funds have that kind of structure. But if we feel like, even if we have those limits, we're going to be shrinking over time, that's not conducive to risk taking.

**n+1:** But I mean you make it sound like people just have to come out to the public and say, "We lost all this money," but the consequences actually would be, ah . . .

**HFM:** There would be some bankruptcies, yeah. And shareholders would be wiped out and management teams would be out on their ear. But that probably should happen. And yeah, there are people in whose interest it is to not recognize the loss and to hope, and to gamble, for resurrection. It's the reason why banks are regulated as heavily as they are—once capitalization gets to zero in the bank, what's the shareholders' incentive? The shareholders' incentive is to gamble for resurrection. He has nothing more to lose; it's only the depositors' money that there is to lose at that point.

**n+1:** Of all the companies in the world, a bank is the least likely to want to go bankrupt.

**HFM:** Yeah, because the whole business model is based on trust, it's based on the appearance of solvency. . . . The kind of structural damage you can do to a bank through bankruptcy is much larger than the damage you can do to a factory if you take it through bankruptcy. So there are reasons that have to do with the fundamentals of business, not just the interests of the management. Banks are going to struggle much harder to avoid admitting that they're bust, and that's why the regulators have to step in and say, "You're bust." Which has happened for IndyMac Bank, a couple of other community banks. FDIC has been taking them over, so you are starting to get that process of recognition.

But we're not at the end of it. One way that people try to get a handle on how big the losses could be is to look at the profits to the financial industry in the U.S. relative to GDP over a long historical period. And you see that as a percentage of GDP it has tended to be pretty stable over time, but over the last five years it became a much larger proportion of GDP. So you just say, "All right, if the true profits that were available really should have just been at the historical trend, how much excess profit was made which really probably needs to be reversed, was really phony-baloney, you know, CDOs, subprime, and all this kind of stuff?" And, if you do that analysis, you get to a number between $1.25 trillion and $1.5 trillion.* The write-downs we've seen so far are on the order of $500 billion, okay? Risk capital has been raised, there's been something like $350 to $400 billion raised; so they've raised new equity to cover those losses. But I think people do that analysis and think, "There must be more, there must be more to go."

**n+1:** You're feeling pretty low?

**HFM:** I'm feeling pretty low, yeah. *Low* is probably the wrong word. I'm feeling pretty nervous and I'm feeling a certain degree of frustration

---

* The IMF in its Global Finance Stability Report (GFSR) published in September 2009 estimated global bank write-downs and charge-offs of $2.8 trillion. In its previous GFSR, published in October 2008, it had estimated that number at $1.4 trillion. The fund deems the process of loss recognition as more advanced in the United States, where 60 percent of eventual total write-downs have already been taken, than in Europe, which has only recognized 40 percent of total losses.

that this situation is stretching on as long as it has, because the losses, the true losses, were inflicted a long time ago, when people built houses they shouldn't have built or built the office park buildings they shouldn't have built or bought cars they couldn't afford. Those losses were created a long time ago.

**n+1:** And then how much, when you're talking about recognizing these losses, how much of that is connected to the real economy and people actually losing their houses?

**HFM:** Some of these houses aren't even occupied. It's just about misallocation of resources, right? I mean, yeah, some of that is people being put in houses they couldn't afford. Now what is this house worth? You sold this to some poor schlub for $400,000 because he was able to get a $400,000 mortgage. His ability to get the mortgage is what created the price. In reality, this guy can afford to carry a mortgage on a $150,000 house, and there's nobody else to buy this house, based on where it's sited and what its features are. And yet if you got to write down the mortgage, you'd have to sell the house out from that person to someone else who can afford that $150,000, or you'd need to come to an agreement with that guy and say, "Look, your payments are now commensurate with a $150,000 mortgage." The loss needs to be recognized. The house isn't worth $400,000; there's a claim on it for $400,000? That claim isn't working. The loss was, the house shouldn't have been built. Now that it's built, what's the maximum value you can get out of it? That's what it's worth.

**n+1:** But how many of these banks that you're talking about, that are not announcing their losses, are looking at people in houses, right? And they don't want to go through a foreclosure?

**HFM:** At the end of the chain, a lot of the time it's securities that are backed by mortgages, yeah. That's probably the biggest single problematic sector. Some of it is commercial lending, some of it is auto loans, some of it is credit cards. What does that mean for credit card loans? What's the loss there? The loss is some iPod was manufactured and was sold to someone for a promise to pay later. On a Visa card. But probably that iPod shouldn't have been made. The metal that makes the case should never have been refined, you know? But what's done is done. The people who have done that have all been paid. So, we need to recognize the loss.

**n+1:** But, you know, some of this is going to mean . . .

**HFM:** That people are kicked out of their homes? Some of it will.

**n+1:** Okay. One more question, a more general question. You know, you have a beautiful mind. I listen to you talk, and then I read over the transcript, and I'm just amazed at the way your mind works. And now we're living through a crisis in capitalism, possibly a really—a historically bad crisis. And do you feel, you know, do you feel that your mind is being used right now in history in the best way it possibly could?

**HFM:** Well, where do you think it would be used better? I mean, I think if there's a problem here, this is the place—this is where the problem is.

# THE COLLAPSE

Three days after the third interview, Fannie Mae and Freddie Mac, who hold a large portion of the many small and now distressed mortgages, go into conservatorship. The next week, Lehman Brothers, the most exposed of the remaining investment banks, begins to totter, its stock price plunging and its leadership desperately scrambling for some kind of rescue. Realizing how bad things might get in the case of a Lehman bankruptcy, Timothy Geithner, president of the New York Federal Reserve Bank, gathers the leaders of the major American and European banks and brokerages to discuss a possible private bailout of Lehman; at the same time, Lehman negotiates to sell part of its business to the English bank Barclays or to Bank of America. After a frantic weekend, the gathered bankers do their part and agree to put up the money, but Bank of America decides to buy the slightly less troubled Merrill Lynch for a hefty $50 billion, and Barclays, needing permission from the British government to purchase Lehman, fails to secure it. Lehman Brothers files for Chapter 11 bankruptcy protection at 1:45 a.m. on September 15.

From: n+1
To: HFM
Date: Mon, Sep 15, 2008, 12:34 p.m.
Subject: holy bejesus!!
    Hang in there, HFM!

From: HFM
To: n+1
Date: Mon, Sep 15, 2008, 12:36 p.m.
Subject: RE: holy bejesus!!
    Seriously. It feels a little like the end of the world.

> BUT!!—this is what I was talking about. Losses need
> to be recognized, corpses taken out for burial. If
> Lehman's demise is handled without total chaos (and
> it feels like it is moving that way), it will be a very
> positive step. If AIG blows up, then you'll find me in
> my bunker. Knock three times in quick succession, or
> you'll get a headful of shotgun pellets.

*AIG is not allowed to go under, instead getting nationalized by the Federal Reserve on September 16 (for $80 billion). But the crisis is far from over. On September 16, the Reserve Primary Fund, one of the largest and oldest money market funds, "breaks the buck." It turns out to have $800 million of exposure to now-worthless Lehman commercial paper. Money market funds face heavy withdrawals and the commercial paper market starts to break down.*

*Stock markets go into uncontained free fall worldwide. Financial companies are the hardest hit, and Morgan Stanley and Goldman Sachs, the two remaining American investment banks, begin to look vulnerable. "Goldman, Morgan Now Stand Alone," says the* Wall Street Journal. *"Fight On or Fold?" Morgan Stanley's clients begin to withdraw billions of dollars in accounts, and its stock plunges.*

*On the evening of September 18, Treasury Secretary Henry Paulson and Federal Reserve Chairman Ben Bernanke meet with congressional leaders to tell them just how bad things are. (The next morning the* Times *describes the congressmen as "stunned.") Paulson and Bernanke present a $700 billion Troubled Asset Relief Program (TARP)— a bailout package for the banks—explaining that if it is not enacted, the consequences will be dire. Leaders from both parties more or less support the plan, but it is met with fierce skepticism from rank-and-file politicians and especially from the citizenry, who consider it a gift to Wall Street of just the sort that people who were losing their homes never got. As the debate over it in Washington heats up, the financial crisis takes over the presidential campaign. In an attempt to demonstrate statesmanship, Republican candidate John McCain, trailing in* the polls, announces that he is going to stop campaigning to devote himself to working on the bailout, and suggests that a scheduled presidential debate be postponed. Obama rebuffs this idea, and the debate proceeds.

On September 21, Morgan Stanley and Goldman Sachs fold, surrendering some of their independence to become bank holding companies—meaning they will from here on out be regulated by the Fed.

On September 26, after ten days of customers withdrawing their deposits in the wake of the Lehman failure, Washington Mutual is seized by federal regulators and sold off to JPMorgan Chase in the largest bank failure in U.S. history.

On September 29, the House of Representatives votes down the TARP proposal from Treasury Secretary Paulson. The S&P 500 falls 9 percent on the news, its largest single-day drop since Black Monday in October 1987. That same day the Treasury offers a guarantee to money market funds, backed by the Exchange Stabilization Fund, a government account intended to intervene in the currency market and to provide financing to foreign governments facing crisis.

As October begins, the crisis spreads. The financial system of Iceland collapses. "Iceland is bankrupt," an economics professor in Iceland tells the New York Times. "The Icelandic krona is history. The only sensible option is for the IMF to come and rescue us." Icelandic banks turn out to have racked up foreign liabilities several times the size of the country's GDP, and the country, until recently rated triple-A, faces the specter of default. Britain experiences a wave of bank failures. Investors continue to flee the Russian stock market, driving it down 70 percent in three months.

October 6–10 is the stock market's worst week since the Great Depression. The Dow Jones loses 22 percent, the S&P 18 percent.

The Federal Reserve attempts to bridge the gap in availability of short-term corporate credit by offering to buy up to $1.3 trillion in commercial paper.

October 23: Alan Greenspan, testifying before Congress, admits that *his commitment to an unfettered free market was "flawed." "I made a mistake in presuming that the self-interests of organizations, specifically banks and others, were such as that they were best capable of protecting their own shareholders and their equity in the firms," Greenspan says.*

*In mid-November, the chairmen of the Big Three automakers—and between them GM and Ford still have $300 billion in revenues, making them the sixth- and seventh-largest U.S. companies, and the second- and third-largest, after Walmart, among companies outside the energy sector—come to Congress asking for $25 billion in bailout money, threatening to go bankrupt if they don't get it.*

*In early December, workers laid off without notice or severance from a door and window factory in Chicago refuse to leave the factory until they are paid. The sit-in lasts six days and garners a great deal of publicity—including the support of President-elect and Vice President-elect Obama and Biden—until the owners of the factory meet their demands for severance payments and other contractual benefits.*

# HFM IV

# HOW BAD IS IT?

*December 11, 2008*
Dow: 8,565.09
Liquid Universe Corporate Index Spread over Benchmark: 535
U.S. OTR ten-year: 0.60 percent
Unemployment: 7.2 percent
Foreclosures: 259,085

**n+1:** Last time we talked it was early September. I walked out of your office. The weather was temperate. I went and got a burger at a place on Third where it seemed like a lot of bankers were also having burgers. No one suspected anything, and the next we know, Fannie Mae and Freddie Mac were bailed out, Lehman was allowed to fail . . . it was early September. So what happened? What was that like?

**HFM:** The Lehman failure was stressful for me personally. We had some exposure to Lehman, very little compared to our exposure to any of our main counterparties, but even for the handful of positions that we had, there's a procedure that you have to go through when a counterparty goes bankrupt in order to close those positions out. I'd never done that before. I don't think anyone here had ever done it before.

And I got it wrong on Lehman. I thought that dealing with the moral hazard issue—that is, not bailing out a bank that was clearly insolvent—was more important than saving it to stabilize the system. And in the first couple of days, the scramble that went on to close out the positions people had with Lehman and, if it was a hedge, to replace them with another hedge went smoother than I thought. There were dislocations, there were some moves in some markets that were clearly related to the rehedging of positions that market participants had with Lehman. But it seemed like it was going okay for a day or two. But then really the effect on confidence manifested itself, and it was very ugly.

**n+1:** At a certain point after Bear went under you had said that there had been speculators who had said Lehman was going to go under, and they handled it.

**HFM:** Their books were pretty rotten, apparently. But they certainly handled the PR a lot better than Bear and kept themselves around longer. And in fact I think there was an opportunity to sell Lehman, but the CEO held out for too much money. They were talking to the Korea Development Bank, apparently they were talking to Barclays, but by the time they advanced that far in those discussions, Lehman was really up against the wall, and Barclays was asking for guarantees from the Treasury or the Fed against losses that they might incur from Lehman's portfolio if they were to take it over. And at that point the Fed or the Treasury, somebody in that complex, maybe everybody, thought that the position of Lehman's books was so bad, was so underwater, that it would be unwise for the Fed or the Treasury to offer those kinds of guarantees.

**n+1:** So things appeared to be going okay with the Lehman bankruptcy, and then it turned out that they weren't.

**HFM:** Yes, it's interesting what happened. It wasn't so much the direct effect of Lehman that caused the markets to have the sort of total seizure that they did for some period in the beginning of October. It was something a little bit more indirect. Lehman was a big issuer of commercial paper—short-dated, unsecured paper—that tends to be bought by money market funds. And money market funds—people treat them like money. We've talked in the past about how the line between what's money and what's a risky asset is sort of a fuzzy line. People tend to regard money market funds as money.

One of the oldest, in fact I think the oldest money market fund, the progenitor of the whole industry, a fund called the Reserve Primary Fund—Primary had meaningful exposure to Lehman paper. Something like 2 percent of that fund was in Lehman paper. When Lehman went under, people who had shares of the Reserve Primary Fund, especially institutional investors who were very much on top of what Primary's holdings were, started to ask for redemptions from that fund. So that led to a run on that money market fund.

As a result, Primary "broke the buck." They had to mark down their Lehman exposure. The holding, the value of one share of the Primary Reserve Fund, was no longer $1—money market funds always try to maintain the value of one share at $1. And that just caused people to—I think the technical term is "lose their shit." People just lost their shit. You thought you had money; now you don't have money. And you don't know how much you have in Reserve Primary Fund, really . . . "We *think* people will recover 98 cents on the dollar, we don't know how long it will take to get people back their money," and suddenly all these money market funds fell under suspicion.* As a result, you worry, "Well, will people take all their money out of money market funds? They're not depositing any money in. The whole commercial paper market may

---

* Shareholders of the Reserve Primary Fund were scheduled to get a fifth distribution of proceeds from the fund's liquidation on October 2, 2009, which would take their total recovery to 91.72 cents on the dollar; $3.5 billion, representing around 5 cents of additional recovery, has been set aside as a special reserve to meet the potential legal costs arising from the tangle of litigation in which the fund finds itself.

grind to a halt." And the commercial paper market is really the life-blood of short-term credit, short-term corporate credit, in this country. Because people don't necessarily sit on piles of ready cash; the way they manage their short-term cash needs is by issuing commercial paper. It's very short-dated, and companies that are of this credit quality generally have no trouble rolling it over. Suddenly there was a question whether the commercial paper market was going to shudder to a halt. And that could lead to very solvent companies . . . not being able to make their payroll, to defaulting. And that means if you're a supplier to a big company, let's say you're a Chinese company exporting to U.S. customers, you're not going to put your goods on a boat if you think the guy on the other end isn't going to be able to pay you. And if you were that importer and you were counting on some sort of letter of credit from a bank, well, the bank's not going to issue a letter of credit because it's worried that the company that it's issuing on behalf of is going to have problems rolling its commercial paper. And maybe that Chinese exporter is worried about the bank too! So trade kind of comes to a halt. It's really a lot like a heart attack. The financial system had a heart attack. But that wasn't because the financial system was reliant on Lehman. It was because the Lehman failure caused a subsequent failure that caused people to question something that was just an unspoken assumption that never really factored in a meaningful way into people's decision calculus.

Now, the Reserve Primary Fund didn't do anything that was inappropriate for a money market fund to do.* But Primary had a reputation for years and years for being the most conservative of the money market funds out there. The manager of that fund had been very vocal about how the other money market funds were taking too many risks, were investing in paper that was a little bit too risky to be appropriate for money market funds. And over time, his

---

* At least not until the week of its unraveling. In May 2009, the SEC filed charges against the operators of the fund for "failing to provide key material facts to investors and trustees about the fund's vulnerability as Lehman Brothers Holdings, Inc. sought bankruptcy protection."

returns lagged against some of his competitors and, I don't know, two years ago, two and a half years ago, three years ago, that fund, Reserve Primary Fund, started getting into riskier pieces of commercial paper. Again, nothing crazy, nothing against the law. I don't think anybody two years ago, or a year ago, or even nine months ago would have said, "Lehman commercial paper, Lehman thirty- and sixty-day commercial paper is inappropriately risky."* But it was still the case that people who know money market funds thought of Primary as the safest, the biggest, the best, and for that fund to break the buck—it was about the least expected thing you can imagine in money market fund land.

In the end, okay, it's 98 cents on the dollar instead of a dollar. But the point is, people then wonder, what other commercial paper do they own? "What's the next surprise I'm going to get? I'm only *earning* 3 percent on this thing. I want my money back." But everyone can't get their money back—the Primary Reserve Fund has it invested in thirty-, sixty-, and ninety-day commercial paper, it takes time for all that paper to mature. A money market fund, like a bank, is not run on the assumption that everyone will want their money back on the same day. Then the Reserve Primary Fund has to say, "We're suspending redemptions, we have to wait for what we own to mature," and *that* freaks people out.

**n+1:** They're standing with pots and pans . . .

**HFM:** Well, in financial centers like New York the average person doesn't cook that much. They get takeout. I don't know if they have pots and pans.

---

* It later came out that Primary loaded up on Lehman commercial paper only after the near-death of Bear Stearns, having witnessed the bailout and concluding that investment bank commercial paper was safer than the market was giving it credit for being. Which was a mistake.

**n+1:** They can bang their Chinese take-out boxes.

**HFM:** Yes, their Chinese menus. Or the extra chopsticks that they accumulate.

**n+1:** So it was really the money market fund that caused—

**HFM:** It caused a lot of damage. It caused the short-term credit markets to seize up, which interfered with trade; it caused forced selling in the stock market, because you have some hedge funds who are dependent on short-term credit, you had people just panicking and taking their money out of mutual funds . . . it just led to, overall, a reevaluation of the line between cash and not-cash.

You know, people tend to talk about money "flowing" from one place to another, but money's not a fluid, it doesn't flow. A better way to think about it is like an exchange rate: What's the exchange rate between risky assets and risk-free assets? Suddenly everybody wanted risk-free assets. They wanted a lot more risk-free assets than they had. And there's only a finite supply at any given point of risk-free assets. So the price of everything risky measured in terms of risk-free assets went way down, pretty abruptly. If all of us said, "I have $10,000 worth of assets in my Fidelity account"—so, stocks, mutual funds, you know, bonds—we think of that as $10,000. If suddenly I said, and you said, and everybody said, "I want ten thousand dollar bills. That's the only thing I think is real money, a dollar bill," what do you think a dollar bill would be worth on the market, in terms of other risky assets? There just aren't enough dollar bills out there for that scenario.

**n+1:** Did you guys start getting calls in . . .

**HFM:** The fund started getting a lot of redemptions. Those have picked up a lot. But that's something that doesn't happen instantaneously, because hedge funds, you can't redeem your money on any given day at a hedge fund. Most hedge funds, the most frequent redemptions are monthly, but more typically quarterly. You have to wait for the quarterly redemption deadline, which is typically the same day for a lot of funds, although usually you have sixty-day advance notice at the end of the quarter. Hedge funds had been experiencing inflows for the last couple of years. This year we started to see redemptions in the hedge fund industry, and it really picked up in the second half of the year. And as we get toward the end of the year, I think the redemptions that are going to be reported are going to be enormous. The hedge fund industry got to something like $2 trillion globally, and if you look at what people in the industry are predicting, next year you're going to be looking at a trillion and a quarter, maybe as low as a trillion.

Some of that is due to investment losses, but a lot of that is redemptions. The interesting thing, much like the Reserve Primary Fund, a hedge fund is not designed to return all of its investors' money at once. And many funds have set redemption terms that assume that a certain number of investors might want to redeem at a given point, but not all of them. And when all the investors come and say, "I want my money back," the funds have to impose restrictions. Those restrictions might be positions that are already envisioned in the fund's by-laws, and there'll be a gate—in any given quarter, only 15 percent of the fund can flow out. Everybody wants their money out, everyone can get 15 percent. Some funds that didn't have any kind of automatic controls on redemptions built into their rules have had to declare essentially *force majeure* and say, "We're suspending redemptions. We can't sell the assets we own quickly enough to meet these redemption requests, so you, Mr. Investor, are stranded with us, and we're going to try and liquidate assets in an orderly fashion and return money to you as we realize it."

Now, that's both stabilizing and destabilizing. It's stabilizing in the sense that if hedge funds had to liquidate all their assets tomorrow, there's just—there aren't enough bids out there for risky assets. You would see the stock market plummet to lows that would make your hair curl; you would see the credit markets just utterly implode, things would be trading for pennies on the dollar, because there's just not enough buying power to absorb all that supply of risky assets. So it's stabilizing to have these curbs on redemptions.

But it's destabilizing in the sense that it creates contagion. Let's take for example an endowment. You're a university endowment and you've placed a lot of money with hedge funds. And you assume that you'll be able to withdraw a certain amount of money every quarter to pay money to support the operations of the university; that's part of the planning you do. Now suddenly the funds you are counting on to be a source of ordinary liquidity have suspended redemptions. What do you do? Well, "What fund *hasn't* suspended redemptions? I'm going to take money from that guy." So it creates contagion between funds.

+ + +

**n+1:** Was the Primary trouble the cause of the liquidity trap you were talking about earlier?

**HFM:** Yes, this is where we're starting to see that the U.S., and maybe the world generally, was falling into a liquidity trap. Everybody wanted risk-free assets, nobody wanted to take any risks, nobody wanted to spend, and that can create a terrible deflationary spiral. Now, the other thing that's happened since the last time we spoke is that the authorities, the treasuries, and finance ministries, not just in the U.S. but worldwide, on the one hand, and monetary authorities on the other hand, like the Fed and central banks around the world, have really wheeled out the big guns. They have taken fairly dramatic action to try to counteract the deflationary and contractionary impact of this sudden surge of risk aversion. So, what kinds of things have you seen? When the commercial paper market seized up, the Fed got involved in literally buying up commercial paper. It has the ability to buy commercial paper. The FDIC and similar organizations worldwide have raised the deposit insurance limit for depositors, so that depositors can feel more comfortable leaving large amounts at banks. And you've seen the TARP, this massive quote-unquote "ballout," whereby the government, the Treasury, has—well, it's said it's going to do a lot of things, but in practice what it's done is it's injected capital into banks, and other countries have done similar things, so that those banks can continue to operate, can continue to take risks, and can bear some losses that they need to bear based on values of risky assets coming down.

Finally, what you're seeing, in the ordinary budget process, is fiscal stimulus—so what Obama's talking about, what several of the EU [European Union] governments are talking about, is spending more. If private demand is falling, they'll try to set it off with public demand.

We'll see if it works or doesn't work.

Now, in terms of inflation, if I had to predict what's going to happen here in the U.S., I think of it as an inflationary U—it's really going to drop. We were running at high inflation because of commodity prices and the economy humming; it's really going to drop because of the financial crisis. And then it will be low for a while. And then one day sentiment will change, and people talk about the Fed having expanded its balance sheet to $2 trillion [from $800 billion], and it has—

**n+1:** They printed it?

**HFM:** They've "printed" it. The banks have crap collateral, and they come to the Fed and say, "I need to borrow against this," and the Fed creates money. Or the Fed basically swaps something like Treasury bills against a risky asset. And thereby the Fed has expanded its balance sheet. And it's done this to the tune of $1.2 trillion, so that the balance sheet is now a little over $2 trillion.

The interesting thing is, where has that money gone? If you look at excess reserves [kept by banks] at the Fed, excess reserves have gone from negligible levels, something on the order of tens of billions of dollars, in 2007, to something like $600 billion. So of the $1.2 trillion in money creation, $600 billion has gone right back to the Fed in excess reserves. Banks are just hoarding the cash. Just like people are hoarding cash. Everybody wants T-bills—T-bills are trading at zero. Obviously that doesn't bespeak a fear of inflation, if people are willing to hold T-Bills at zero.

**n+1:** Weren't the banks given money so that they could give it out to people, and now they're hoarding it?

**HFM:** But they're hoarding it in a precautionary way, they don't know what the call is going to be on their cash. Economic agents all across the board have built up a lot of precautionary liquidity. The Fed can create tons of liquidity but it doesn't really get into the economy, it doesn't really stimulate economic activity, because it winds up being built up as precautionary balances, which in practical terms means a lot of it ends up as excess reserves back in the Fed.

What's scary is the day that people say, "You know what, I'm going to use that liquidity," and there are a couple of aspects of this that scare me, that are particular to this crisis. Number one is, let me tell you, there is like no investing going on, right? Companies aren't investing. Hedge funds aren't investing. Investment in the real economy has fallen a lot. So when a year or two or three years down the road, suddenly demand perks up again very quickly—well, nobody's been drilling oil wells, nobody's been building steel plants, nobody's been expanding their mines, and you could find yourself in a situation where very quickly the economy runs up against supply constraints. So that could intensify the inflationary spike. Right now there's a lot of slack in the economy, people are worried about it, but the supply curve might not move that much for a couple of years because there's no investment going on.

+++

**n+1:** Can we go back a little bit to AIG? When we were emailing about this a while back, AIG was the thing that really freaked you out.

**HFM:** AIG did freak me out.

**n+1:** Why is that?

**HFM:** AIG freaked me out for the reason that there would be a lot of contagion by AIG because AIG was such a large counterparty to other institutions, such that if AIG failed, other institutions would suddenly become suspect. If AIG fails, with Goldman hedging so much of its credit risk with AIG, then is Goldman safe? Not unlike when Lehman failed and it caused Reserve Primary to break the buck, it would create a wave of suspicion. I think it would have been just as bad as Lehman if AIG failed.

I also thought the government bailing out AIG, there was a good chance that that would be an okay trade for the government. Because AIG is a constellation of businesses, many of which are very valuable and pretty safe franchise businesses. Like life insurance, for instance. These are highly regulated, there's nothing wrong with them, they're difficult franchises to build, in total it's worth a lot. In a normal environment there would be eager buyers for those businesses.

The business that took AIG down was this financial products business, which was really kind of like a hedge fund. But it was only one way, it wasn't hedged, it was just underwriting a lot of credit risk. And using AIG's high rating to say, "I'm going to write credit insurance to everybody, and I'm not going to post any collateral because I'm so high-rated, counterparties can treat an uncollateralized hedge with

AIG as money-good." As it turned out, it wrote so much of this, on so many correlated risks—correlated risks that would only become effective in a very, very extreme scenario—that when that extreme scenario happened, the losses were enormous.

Now, again, in an ordinary environment, its other businesses would be worth so much that AIG, given time, would be able to sell those businesses down and raise enough money to plug the hole at the financial products unit. The problem was that it didn't have months to do that. Once it lost its high credit rating, it had to post collateral immediately—and that was just liquidity it didn't have. So it seems to me that it was a good trade for the government, because the government has all the time in the world to dispose of those businesses.\* Unfortunately in this environment there isn't really a bid for those businesses, so the government's going to have to wait a long while, because every financial company is in some way or another under suspicion, every financial company's stock is worth less.

**n+1:** Are you rooting for the government?

**HFM:** I'm a taxpayer. I think if the government is going to lay out money to buy these companies, hopefully the bailouts are profitable, just like the Chrysler bailout was profitable [in the early 1980s]. The mistake that people make is they talk about the TARP, right, it's going to be $700 billion, we're spending $700 billion to bail out Wall Street or the financial system. Well, you're not spending $700 billion, you're investing $700 billion in trades that no private investor would go in on those terms, because, you know, it *is* a subsidy, the government is lending at lower rates than a private investor would, or asking for less

---

\* In March 2009, the Fed and Treasury came up with a third expansion of the AIG bailout, lowering the interest rate on its loans from the government and injecting another $30 billion of TARP funds, making a positive financial outcome for government look most unlikely.

equity upside than a private investor would, or because no private investor is big enough to make that investment.

But it's still an investment. So even if you think that these investments are a bad deal, they're likely to lose money, they're still not going to lose 100 cents on the dollar. So the government is making these equity injections into preferreds of Citibank; those aren't worth zero, they're worth something. And it's very likely that, five years out, they're worth as much as the government put in. Now, the government might make an annualized return of 5 percent on that. No private investor would have made an investment on those terms. If the government wanted to be totally commercial about it, they could have driven a harder bargain, or it could have invested in other stuff. But if you're asking if the government is actually going to lose money on these trades, it's not clear at all that the government is going to lose any money. It will probably lose some, but it's not for certain.*

**n+1:** When you talk about AIG insuring credit instruments . . .

**HFM:** Let's say you're Goldman. Goldman buys some mortgage-backed paper. They buy some senior tranches of a mortgage-backed securitization. Now Goldman says, "You know what, we own this, now we've decided that we don't want to take this credit risk, or we want to lay some off, we want to keep some for ourselves and lay some off." How do they do that? They can actually sell the instrument itself

---

* The Congressional Budget Office publishes periodic reports on the fiscal impact of the TARP. The June 2009 report pegs the estimated subsidy of the program at $159 billion, but this estimate compares the return of TARP outlays against what investments on market terms would have yielded, rather than the absolute cost (www.cbo.gov/ftpdocs/100xx/doc10056/06-29-TARP.pdf). According to data from the Treasury's Office of Financial Stability, the Capital Purchase Program (CPP), the part of the TARP dedicated to putting equity into financial institutions, has realized a profit on the first set of investments that banks have repaid. Obviously, only the healthiest banks have the wherewithal to so quickly repay the Treasury, so they do not constitute a representative sample of the program. However, these banks do represent over one-third of the total outlays under the CPP, so it's not chump change either.

for cash. Or they can enter into a credit swap with a counterparty, where the counterparty will pay Goldman if this security defaults.

**n+1:** This is a credit default swap.

**HFM:** Yes. Now, if AIG were not a highly rated counterparty . . . let's say it was a hedge fund that Goldman was getting this protection from. For Goldman's auditors to truly consider that Goldman had laid off this risk, Goldman would have to take some collateral from that hedge fund, so that if the hedge fund goes bust, Goldman has enough money to go out and buy protection on that security, even if the cost of protection has jumped higher. And every time the security goes down in value, the hedge fund would have to post more collateral, because the risk of default is higher, and the value of the credit default swap is higher.

AIG did not have to post collateral, because AIG was a very, very highly rated creditor. So the auditors say, "Well, that's fine, you don't have to take cash from AIG. A promise from AIG is basically as good as cash."*

What happened is, AIG had written so much of this insurance, and it turned out to be so correlated, that the portfolio was deeply, deeply in the money for its counterparties and against AIG. And when AIG's credit rating fell, suddenly its counterparties were entitled to ask for collateral. It was just too much cash for AIG to come up with in a short period of time.

**n+1:** So it wasn't clear that it was going to blow up in their faces?

---

* It should be said that AIG wouldn't have a business if it reserved enough capital against each contract so that it could pay off all the contracts if they all went against AIG at once. The premiums are just too low. The only way AIG can earn an adequate return on capital is to calculate how much capital it will reserve against each contract under the assumption that the likelihood of each individual contract going against it is small and that the correlation between these loss events is very low.

**HFM:** Oh, they wouldn't have done it if it was clear it was going to blow up in their faces. In retrospect, people say, "That's crazy. How can you assume that in an economic downturn we're not going to see a chain reaction, where a lot of these subprime mortgages go bust, houses get foreclosed on, property values fall, that causes more people to have negative equity, they default?" And there is a whole lot of correlation. But if you look at historical data, at the time it didn't look like correlation was that high.

But look, there were many people who thought that correlation was high, or would be high, and who made a lot of money betting on that. There are a few hedge funds that have done well in the last year or two, or hedge funds that bet aggressively on that very proposition.

**n+1:** There was an article in *Portfolio* about a guy who was short this stuff.*

**HFM:** [David] Einhorn? He's a smart guy. He was short Lehman, all the financial stuff. He's doing poorly this year, though.†

I think at AIG and at some of these investment banks, there were people who were doing these securitizations who knew that ultimately they were going to blow up, and they didn't care. They didn't care because the structure of compensation at a place like AIG and certainly at the investment banks leads people to take a future-discounting model, that's what I'd call it. There's this year's compensation period . . . and then there's the future. And the future is *very* heavily discounted. And many of these risks, like the risk of an economic shock grave enough to cause these brittle subprime securitizations to break, was something you wouldn't expect to happen every year, it would take a couple of years, and because people were paid according to mark-to-market profits in a given year, they continued to do this business

---

\* Michael Lewis, "The End," *Portfolio*, November 2008.

† Einhorn's fund, Greenlight, was apparently down 22 percent in 2008 but has had a stellar 2009.

even though they knew that it was storing up risks for an eventual meltdown. That's true of AIG and that's true of the investment banks.

Now, I haven't spoken to anyone who said to me, "Oh yeah, I knew, and I just kept printing these trades, because I figured the clock hadn't struck midnight." Perhaps they wouldn't admit that to me.*

+++

**n+1:** So the stock market has collapsed. You've talked about the financial markets being a reflection of the real economy, but the real economy doesn't necessarily have to reflect the financial markets, does it?

**HFM:** It doesn't have to, but it's circular. Financial variables are a way of accounting for what's going on in the real world. But the real world itself starts to react to financial variables if they're extreme enough. And it's funny—the financial system, all the big guns that have been wheeled out by the government and the monetary authorities, have in the last couple weeks kind of stabilized what gets called the "guts" of the financial market. There is short-term credit, there is a certain degree of lending between banks, corporates are able to get their commercial paper rolled over, for the most part. So it's functioning—in a much reduced fashion, there are surprises and shocks every day, but it hasn't ground to a complete halt. But now you are seeing the effect on the real economy. So what's happening? We have the largest one-

---

* In the end, AIG paid approximately $50 billion to counterparties on the other end of its credit default contracts, with Goldman Sachs at the top of the list of payees. The Treasury suspected this was too much—that the payouts could have been mitigated—and launched an investigation. Goldman, meanwhile, has insisted it derived no benefit from the AIG rescue, because the bank had fully hedged its exposure to the insurer through buying credit default swaps on AIG from other counterparties. That may be so, but it neatly skirts the question of whether those counterparties would have been in any shape to make good on the contracts in a world where AIG had suddenly gone bust. It also doesn't change the ultimate cost to U.S. taxpayers one iota.

month drop in payrolls in twenty-five years. You're starting to see real job loss. You're starting to see actual companies going out of business, or high-profile default. A good example is Tribune Corp.* So you are starting to see the effect on the real economy.

Some of that impact is not a direct impact of the financial markets, but it's the hangover from the misallocation of resources, which is the same thing that's causing problems in the financial markets. Whereas a pure impact of the financial markets is where people look at their 401(k)s and say, "Gosh, I don't want to spend." That's a pure impact of financial variables causing people's attitudes to change, changing their risk tolerance, their propensity to consume.

**n+1:** So how bad are things right now?

**HFM:** In the financial market things seem to be scraping along at the bottom. I don't open my eyes every day and expect to be hit in the face with a brick. Which is the way it felt for part of October.

But now what everybody's looking at is what is the impact going to be on the real economy. The S&P today, it's back where we were—it's been a very bumpy journey, but we're not lower than we were back in October. So the idea that the financial markets are a one-way bet that just go down every day, that idea is behind us, at least for the moment.

What you hear about is: Is unemployment going to peak at 8 percent? At 10 percent? Or is it going to go higher than that? What's being priced in by the financial markets is very high, and I think that's just because of the liquidation of credit portfolios, the hedge funds having to liquidate and sell down their positions, and the loss of leverage in general is forcing people to sell down their positions,

---

* Investor Sam Zell bought out the *Tribune* in late 2007 with a lot of borrowed money, so it was ultimately a pretty fragile deal. A downturn in the advertising market in late 2008 sank it very quickly.

so I don't think anyone thinks the default rates are going to be as high as bond prices imply. But how high are they really going to be? We don't know.

One thing is when the short-term credit market ground to a halt [in October], a huge percentage of the bulk cargo ship fleet just went idle. Trade just wasn't happening. It felt apocalyptic. The system had ground to a halt. Now you're getting the hangover of that. Companies that had to stop operating for a month—they don't go belly-up immediately, but now you're seeing they're starting to have layoffs, their suppliers are having problems, and their suppliers are having layoffs. The auto companies are a great example. They've been in trouble for a long time, but car sales in October were down like 40 percent year to year, and that was because people were like, "Gee, I don't know if I'm going to lose my job, I don't know if I can get a car loan, I don't know what's going to happen, I'm just not buying a car." And now you see the impact of that. The car companies went from limping along in precarious shape to being in a position where they can be out of business if they don't get an extraordinary infusion of resources from the government by year-end.

**n+1:** And it's happening quite quickly.

**HFM:** The linkages? It is moving quickly. I think you'd rather that it happened quickly than it being slow and writhing. And particularly if the government is already responding. But it's certainly traumatic. It's not fun.

**n+1:** And if the cargo ships weren't moving, does that mean there weren't products on shelves?

**HFM:** I think there were instances where the supply chains broke down. I don't think it got to the point where there weren't products on shelves. But I'll tell you this: I've done a lot of agriculture over the years, it's one area I've got investments. There are farmers who weren't able to buy fertilizer. So plantings are way down. You may see the impact of that in a year. Now, obviously commodity prices are way down, so it sort of counteracts, but the point is, yeah, less is going to be produced, because the credit chain and the supply chain broke down. In the U.S. there were problems with getting enough propane to grain silos to dry the grain going into the silos. Again, because of credit issues. You don't see that immediately, because that's still pretty far from the shelves, but it may have an impact on prices months from now.

**n+1:** Of bread?

**HFM:** Yeah.

**n+1:** So who's not getting credit there? Aren't the farmers good for it?

**HFM:** Well, since crop prices have fallen a lot—there was a bubble and then they fell—suddenly people are worried about farmers' credit. Or the bank that was extending the credit to the farmers might be worried about its own financial strength, and it wants to lend less, because it's trying to hoard liquidity.

**n+1:** But it's not even—it's not even—it's just a lot of worrying . . .

**HFM:** Yeah, it's risk aversion! And it sounds so crazy, that a huge economy, I mean bricks, and mortar, and steel, works or doesn't work because a few people have some deficit or excess of neurotransmitters in their brain. It sounds crazy! But that's exactly what it is.

This is not a crisis that was caused because there was a drought, or because a meteor hit London and obliterated it, or because there was a war that destroyed productive capacity. This is because there was a misallocation of resources, because people had too much of that neurotransmitter in their brain, that then caused them to have too little of it, and now all they want are risk-free assets, and that causes the machinery of finance to really shudder to a halt.

Because financial decision making is about risk. What you do when you're trading is apportioning risk. It's about moving consumption from today to tomorrow, or vice versa, and about the risk associated with that, about transferring the risk associated with that. If nobody wants to take the risk, then nothing happens.

You know, it's easy to understand how living standards would go down if somebody bombed all the factories in America. What's kind of hard to get your head around is that those factories are still there! All that good stuff we were buying, there's still the capacity to make it. But somehow it's not getting done, because people's attitudes about risk have changed. And as long as I've been in the financial markets, that's still crazy and awesome and hard to get your head around.

+++

**n+1:** What was the scariest moment of the past two months?

**HFM:** I think the scariest moment of the past two months was when the TARP was being voted on in Congress, and we had the TV on here, we were watching—and the financial markets had really been beaten up, and credit spreads had really widened out, and the financial system really couldn't function. And they had come back during the day because it looked like TARP was going to pass, and so we're watching the TV—

**n+1:** You got rid of the TVs.

**HFM:** We have one TV on another floor, and so we went down to this other floor and watched on this one TV that we have. And when they announced that it wasn't passing, it was scary. It was like, "These guys just do not understand the gravity of the situation."

And it was also very frustrating, because in the back of my head I felt like, "Well, probably this will get done, this bill will get passed, but the benefit that it's going to have, because ultimately what you need to do is restore confidence, the benefit is going to be vitiated by the fact that it was passed in this messy way." I think there's an old Latin saying, "He gives twice who gives quickly." If you give in a very reluctant and recalcitrant way, it's not as much of a gift as when you say, you know, "Here it is." The way that it was passed, I think, took away a good deal of the benefit of the package. So that moment was pretty scary.

There was another moment when Citibank, even after its initial equity injection, its stock was down to something like three and a half dollars, it looked like Citibank might go down. If Citibank went down—you think that's one of the banks that the government is going to backstop it, it's too big to fail, and people were *still* selling down the stock. That day I had to go out of the office for a meeting and I ran into a colleague of mine coming back to the office and I asked him, you know, "Where have you been?" And he said, "I went to Citibank to withdraw my deposits."

This is a professional investor, right? He should be calm, cool, and collected. And I thought, "Gosh, if a professional investor is going and taking his money out of Citibank, this is serious." And I think the amount of money he had in the bank was less than the amount insured by the government. It was just pure blind fear.

Then they got another equity injection, and it's still not doing fantastic, but I don't think anybody's talking about its potential failure.*

**n+1:** So what's going to happen now?

---

* Citi was hardly out of the woods, but rather than talking about outright failure, the market came to worry about nationalization. In February 2009, the government agreed to a third rescue package, with the U.S. government converting its preferred shares into common equity. The government ended up owning a third of the company. Its stock dipped below $1 at the beginning of March 2009, and was trading at around $3.35 in December 2009.

**HFM:** I think the financial markets will probably be reasonably stable through year-end. You can tell things are slowing down at the moment. What we're going to see is the ramifications into the real market. So we'll probably see more unemployment, we'll certainly see more bankruptcies. You know what it's like? It's like somebody drops a depth charge onto a submarine, and you hear a big explosion, but you don't know what's happening. Like, a little while later bodies start to bob up? We're waiting for the bodies to bob up.

Meanwhile, the U.S. government has extended so much aid to various other sectors of the economy, and it's expected to have to do more, that now people are worried about U.S. credit. To buy credit protection on U.S. government debt now costs you more than to buy credit protection on Campbell's soup! But, I mean, buying credit protection on the U.S., it's sort of a mind-bending concept. The U.S. only issues in dollars; it only issues in its own currency. More importantly, from whom are you going to buy protection on the U.S. government's credit? I mean, if the U.S. government defaults, *what bank* is going to be able to make good on that contract? Who are you going to buy that contract from, the Martians? Sometimes I think it would be great if this Mars lander actually discovered life on Mars—we could start trading with them. Somebody finally would be uncorrelated enough, we could buy protection from them on the U.S. government and feel like they could actually pay it back. LGM Capital Management, Little Green Men Capital Management, a perfectly good counterparty.

**n+1:** Holiday party this week?

**HFM:** We're not going to have a holiday party. We're having holiday "drinks." Which is good. I'm anti-holiday-party. I sit with these people all day long, I don't need to spend any more time with them. And people always get too drunk—and something bad happens.

*The crisis continues. The government is now buying shares of American banks at a rate of approximately $10 billion a month.*

*In mid-December, a prominent Wall Street trader named Bernard Madoff is arrested for large-scale fraud.*

*The* Wall Street Journal *reports that Merrill Lynch executives received $3.5 billion in bonuses at the end of 2008—a year in which the firm's losses were a staggering $27 billion.*

# HFM V
# YEAR-END CLOSING

January 16, 2009
Dow: 8,281.22
Liquid Universe Corporate Index Spread over Benchmark: 467
U.S. OTR ten-year: 2.31 percent
Unemployment: 7.6 percent
Foreclosures: 303,410

**n+1:** So you spent the last part of the year closing down the books—is that what it's called?

**HFM:** Closing the books for the year, which really mainly relates to getting prices for all of the securities, instruments, derivatives in our book so that our year-end financials are totally accurate. It's actually the worst: A lot of banks don't close their books for the year on the calendar year, they have a fiscal year, but our fiscal year is the calendar year, and there literally is no day of the year that is worse for the process of getting marks for your whole portfolio than December 31, because everyone is gone. You're looking for a price on an illiquid security and you call up the bank you dealt with, and the salesperson you deal with is not there, his backup's not there, his backup's backup is not there, the trader's backup is not there, you're literally getting the most junior person on the desk trying to get someone on his cell phone on the ski slope in Vermont—it's just about the dumbest time to choose to do it. Every year, two weeks in advance, I send a list to all my counterparties, saying, "Here's the list of things I need pricing for, really, make sure you have somebody available to price these. And 'skiing' is not an excuse; 'I'm with my family on safari, climbing Mt. Kilimanjaro'—not an excuse." And every year the excuses are, "I'm skiing," or the guy's on safari, whatever—it's incredible. So my New Year's is always wrecked. I'm waiting around for the last guy to give me the last price.

**n+1:** Do all hedge funds do this?

**HFM:** All financial institutions have to do this, but banks have more of an infrastructure for it. Hedge funds, we're more leanly staffed, and it falls more to the portfolio manager.

**n+1:** And on top of that you saw all the staggering losses?

**HFM:** No, we mark things to market every day. So we know. And our losses weren't staggering. But we knew our returns, which were in fact negative, but not dramatically so, every day, with a high degree of accuracy.

**n+1:** Was this the worst year you've seen?

**HFM:** It's the worst year *I've* ever had. But the funny thing is, since year-end I've had some meetings with investors, and they've said, "Oh, you guys put in a decent performance," which tells you how bad it must be other places.

**n+1:** What did you lose on in particular? Can you talk about that?

**HFM:** All sorts of things, really. This was a year where any trade you had on that other hedge funds had on, that was a popular hedge fund trade, performed poorly because there were other hedge funds that were forced to unwind that trade. So we suffered a little bit from that, though those are losses that I think we'll make back.

**n+1:** What was a popular hedge fund trade?

**HFM:** Let's see . . . a trade that a lot of hedge funds had on, maybe not at the end of the year but during the year, was they were short the most junior tranches of subprime mortgage securitizations, because they thought that was going to go really terribly. So they were long the senior tranches many times the amount that they were short the more junior tranches. Because, you know, "What's going to happen is the junior tranches will be utterly destroyed, and the senior tranches will decline maybe a little bit, but I can kind of make the trade so that it's carry-neutral." And the assumption is that the senior tranches will be much less sensitive, will move a lot less. But what happened is that because every hedge fund had that trade on, or so many hedge funds had that trade on, and had to liquidate, that meant that the junior tranches actually performed less poorly than they would have, because people had to buy them back, and the senior tranches got utterly destroyed.

Now, the root of the problem in subprime was an underestimate of the deterioration in the housing market. But the size of the move in the trade was massively amplified by the fact that so many funds had it on. So when a few funds were forced by losses to take it off, that pushed the trade further into negative territory, inflicting worse losses on other funds, who in turn needed to liquidate, and so on. So if you were in that crowded trade, you got hurt pretty badly.

The other thing that hurt people was any trade that relied on a high degree of leverage, trades that relied on receiving financing for that trade from banks, those got hurt because banks were cutting financing.

And I think finally just credit trades—trades making bets on credit—credit did really, really poorly. If you were long credit at all, you got hosed.

**n+1:** How come you guys didn't do as badly as other places?

**HFM:** I think it's because we tend to run our book more neutral to obvious economic factors. We're never very long or very short credit; we tend to be looking for relative value in trades. And we got hurt because some of those relative value trades are popular hedge fund trades and many of them rely on financing. But we didn't make huge outright macroeconomic bets that have the potential to go very wrong in an environment as chaotic as the one we saw this year.

**n+1:** And have your redemptions been worse or better or the same as others'?

**HFM:** They've been the same, but I think the reasons for those redemptions have changed. I think at first they had to do with performance—with the fact that our performance was mediocre in '07. We made money but we underperformed some of our peers, so those redemptions related simply to us. What's happened now is that investors are actually reasonably happy with our performance, but they need to leave. They were counting on income from other funds that's not there, or they were counting on the ability to redeem from other funds, and those funds have suspended their redemptions. So, much as a hedge fund when it's in trouble tends to sell what it can, not what it wants to, investors in hedge funds when they're facing a situation where they can't get their money out of a lot of funds, they get liquidity where they can, not where they want to. And since we remain very liquid and continue to return money to people who ask for it, people come to us for redemptions even if they're not displeased with our performance. It's kind of perverse, actually.

**n+1:** And this means you have to get out of trades?

**HFM:** It means we have to get out of trades. Luckily we've always run with a lot of excess liquidity, so we haven't really had to scramble to unwind anything. Our book has certainly shrunk, but we've been able to do that by natural attrition, things maturing, and we haven't had to scramble to get out of any trades. It's something that's cost us in good years—the fact that we ran it with so much excess liquidity, it dampened our returns—but it's paid off in bad years.

**n+1:** You've had pretty serious layoffs.

**HFM:** We've fired a lot of people. I hate all the mumbo-jumbo terms people use. The last one I heard was "involuntary redundancy"—someone had ended up in involuntary redundancy. I like to say we fired people. We fired people. Yes, we did.

**n+1:** What proportion?

**HFM:** About 35 percent, compared to our peak at the end of 2007.

**n+1:** And is that exactly in line with your losses?

**HFM:** That is a little bit less than our losses plus our redemptions. I always felt we were a little bit bloated to begin with. And even if we hadn't had redemptions or losses, I thought we needed fewer people. When you have a very lucrative business model like a hedge fund, there's not a tremendous amount of pressure—particularly if the owner of the fund, the partners of the fund, are not very greedy people, and I think that's the case for us, we're not particularly greedy—it's easier to run with more people.

**n+1:** What was the kind of principle by which you . . . I mean, 35 percent, that's a lot of people. How did you do that?

**HFM:** Have you read Shirley Jackson's story "The Lottery"?

**n+1:** [*laughs uncomfortably, not because HFM is randomly firing 35 percent of his company, but because he has not read this famous short story*]

**HFM:** No, really, there are two different kinds of firings. Well, three: one is if someone's no good and you fire him, but you should be doing that all the time. But in respect to shrinking your head count to become more efficient, there are sort of two ways to go. One is there were departments or areas that we thought were overstaffed, and the productivity was too low, nobody had demanded efficiency of those areas, and that was the fault of the top managers. Because they'd said, "We need to produce X, and I don't care how many people you need to throw at the problem"—so there's improving efficiency in those areas. And then there were certain businesses or functions that we just didn't want to do anymore. So we just shut those down entirely. I would say it was about half and half.

**n+1:** You were talking last time after we turned off the tape that there was just a problem with the pay structure.

**HFM:** Well, I don't think we've cracked that nut entirely, but the landscape of the labor market has changed tremendously, and people *know* that jobs are harder to come by, and so that makes them commensurably less demanding, and that allows us to pay smaller bonuses where that's appropriate and not worry so much about the competitive consequences. You hear all these stories about the banks, and the banks are often the benchmark for what more junior people at hedge funds get paid. The comparison that you make is, "What would a third-year analyst or a second-year associate or a VP at a bank make?" and we have good numbers on that, and those numbers are down. The employees make comparisons to that, so if we pay people less because we think they deserve less, we're not going to lose people, because (a) nobody's hiring, and (b) they can see that those comparator numbers are lower.

**n+1:** What was the situation before this whole thing blew up?

**HFM:** Before the labor market changed? Look, bubbles create other bubbles, they're like derivative bubbles, so to the extent that there was a bubble in credit or a bubble in the mortgage market, that created a bubble for people who could trade those products. There was just a misallocation of resources not only into mortgages, let's say, but also into the trading of mortgages, and it sucked talent into those areas that probably should be deployed other places. And the way talent gets sucked into those places is by a price signal, the compensation going out. The pay scale for finance was just—incredibly out of whack. You had guys who were literally just a couple of years out of college, maybe they'd done a year or two at an investment bank, making several hundred thousand dollars a year doing pretty low-value-added Excel modeling tasks.

**n+1:** What does that mean?

**HFM:** They do financial models on Excel.

**n+1:** I know Excel.

**HFM:** It was kind of crazy what people were being paid. And for the more senior people, the kind of deals they were getting—because their pay tends to be not just a number range but a percentage of the profits they generate—they were getting very high percentages of the profits, and very high guarantees. To get somebody with experience to come to a fund you had to guarantee them a pretty high number. And the decision to pay those kinds of numbers was motivated by the fact that other places were paying those kinds of numbers, and their ability to pay those kinds of numbers was motivated by the fact that there were *huge* amounts of assets coming into hedge funds, and hedge funds are able to charge a management fee for the assets under management. So if you had tons of assets coming in, you needed people to manage those assets, you had to get quality people, you had a ton of money to spend, and everybody was looking for people qualified to work at a hedge fund—there was just tremendous competition for those people, and it drove prices to ridiculous levels. And it changed people's attitudes—I mean, there was a palpable cockiness that one sensed from employees. And there was a lack of distinction, I think, between people who were really good, who you would want in any environment, and people who you could just fill a seat with because they had a résumé that stamped them as minimally qualified.

**n+1:** And was there a point where you noticed this happening?

**HFM:** It's been building over the years. The craziest it became was probably post-2005, and continued in 2006, and then started to ebb in 2007 because we did start running into problems in 2007, and 2008 has turned it around 180 degrees. Look, as a boss it's kind of a good thing: You can really upgrade your talent, you can distinguish between good performers and poor performers a lot more sharply than when the price to get somebody to show up is some ridiculous amount of money. And it's society-wide—I mean, it's funny, I worked in finance through the Internet boom, right? And the Internet boom, it was the same thing, it was like a price signal pulling people into a sector, because it was evident to people how much money you could make if you created CheeseSand-wich.com and sold it for a couple of million. It was like an exodus from finance—I can't tell you how many times I would call up to do a trade and someone would say, "Oh yeah, this trader, he quit, he's going to join a friend at an Internet start-up." And then the Internet bubble popped and all those people kind of filtered back into finance.

Then finance started sucking people from all over. You'd walk around our trading floor and there were guys who were math Ph.D.s and physics Ph.D.s, and chemists, and lawyers, and doctors—there were *doctors* on our trading floor, who trade, you know, the health care sector. The bubble in financial assets had a derivative bubble in people. There was a misallocation of financial resources and a mis-allocation of people resources. And the reversion of that bubble in the price of financial assets will lead to a reversion of that bubble in human resources. That's a good thing, you know? Some of these physicists should be doing physics; some of these computer scientists should be doing computer science. Doctors should be curing people! It's not a bad thing.

**n+1:** If someone had had a heart attack on the trading floor, you could have—

**HFM:** You know, they really don't like it when you ask them to diagnose you. If you're like, "You know, I have a stomachache, and, uh . . . ," they don't like that.

+ + +

**n+1:** We've talked a lot about the misallocation of resources—and you talked about how the factories are still there, and we can still make a lot of the stuff. But wasn't a lot of that stuff . . . .

**HFM:** Some of the stuff was stuff people didn't want.

**n+1:** Or need!

**HFM:** Some of the stuff was just unsellable and should never have been manufactured. Like houses in places where nobody wants to live. Autos, though, are an interesting case. Was there too much capacity in the auto industry? I don't know, perhaps there was too much capacity in the auto industry. But there wasn't *twice* as much capacity as there ought to have been. But auto sales are down on the order of 50 percent, because people aren't able to get credit to buy cars. That's not a case of capacity that never should have been there—the fall in demand far outstrips what you would have suspected if it was just a question of misallocation of productive capacity.

**n+1:** So you don't think we have a problem with people buying a new car too often?

**HFM:** Well, look, it depends on what you mean by too often. If we're talking in the Al Gore discourse, I have nothing to say about that— that's not my area, I'm not an expert. But if you're just talking about how often people wanted to buy a new car and how often they could afford to buy a new car, then, yeah, there probably was credit too readily available, and there were probably people buying cars with loans that they would never really be able to pay back. But not *half* the people buying cars.

**n+1:** How big a deal is it if the Detroit carmakers go under?

**HFM:** It's less big a deal than if a bank goes under. Because, look, we have a bankruptcy regime that is well suited to deal with industrial companies. The problem with Detroit is that these companies are overindebted, and they have some contracts that are no longer economically tenable, or maybe they never were economically tenable. But there's still value in those factories—you just have to reduce the claims on them. And now these companies have gone bankrupt, though this is happening without a bankruptcy: Debt holders are negotiating to reduce their claims, equity holders are being largely wiped out, and these contracts are being renegotiated. If the companies were to go through bankruptcy, the exact same thing would happen.

It's interesting to note what the auto executives did in communicating to the country the consequences of bankruptcy—it was tremendously, tremendously irresponsible. The executives of these companies went with their hats in hand to Congress and said, "If we go through Chapter 11, it's not just a question of reorganizing; these companies are going to disappear. There's going to be real physical damage done. Because no one would be crazy enough to buy a car from a company that's about to go through bankruptcy or is going through bankruptcy." Before they spoke, I think there were plenty of people who would buy a car from a company going through bankruptcy; people buy plane tickets from airlines that are *in* bankruptcy *all the time.* But after an executive goes on TV and says, "Well, no one would be crazy enough to buy a car from a company going through bankruptcy," then no one *will* be crazy enough to buy a car from a company going through bankruptcy. And that's tremendously irresponsible on the part of these executives, because they have a duty, and the boards of these companies have a duty, when their companies go into the zone of insolvency, not just to the shareholders but also to the creditors. And to say that the company will be utterly destroyed by bankruptcy filing—and to make statements that will bring that about!—is tremendously disruptive to the value of the debts that those creditors hold. It's really like playing chicken: "Either this company is going to avoid bankruptcy, or I'm going to burn the whole thing down."

**n+1:** What's the next industry that's going to be in trouble?

**HFM:** I don't know. I think the industry that's actually really in trouble now is municipal and state government. The financial situation of the states and the municipalities is deteriorating very fast. I'm not telling you anything particularly insightful, because if you look at where credit spreads are on the state and municipal default swap market, they've widened out tremendously. But I think that's probably where there's going to be a lot of pain, a lot of layoffs, hiring freezes, salary reductions—all the kinds of things that we're seeing in companies.

+ + +

**n+1:** We're about to have a new administration. If Tim Geithner gets tripped up by tax returns and nannies [like some of Obama's other nominees], and Obama's like, "HFM, I've been reading your interviews, you can remain anonymous but I want you to take over the Treasury or the Fed," which one would you take over?

**HFM:** Oh, there's not enough money in the world to get me to take either of those jobs. They're going to be horribly difficult jobs, both the Fed and Treasury. And Tim Geithner I happen to know a little bit—when he was at the IMF, I had some limited interactions with him on some things—and he was a stubborn son of a bitch, really hard to deal with, but very smart, and thoughtful. But stubborn. I think he'll be very good in the role. But it's going to be a terrible job: All you're going to be doing is dealing with crises, telling people things they don't want to hear. And the Fed—I mean, Bernanke's term isn't up for a while, but I wouldn't want to be in his shoes. He's got Larry Summers sitting in the wings, basically lurking, waiting for the term to be up.* And whoever's sitting there will be at a Fed that's had its balance sheet massively expanded, that's had the tasks

---

* Bernanke's shoes became more comfortable at the end of August 2009, when President Obama appointed him to a second term as Fed chairman.

that it's responsible for massively expanded. It's sitting on a portfolio of all kinds of credit product that it's never allowed on its balance sheet before, the value of which is very uncertain. It's a terrible job, who wants that job? But this is a hypothetical, go ahead.

**n+1:** Okay. Given the full resources of the U.S. government, what would you do right now?

**HFM:** I think what they're doing, what they've done, is along the right lines. What they got wrong was the sequencing; that was a huge issue, and they're now kind of getting on the right side of that. What do I mean? In October, it was like a patient having a heart attack: the short-term credit market ceased to function. That's the heart of our economic system; it ceased to function. The government was like the doctor. The government runs into the heart attack patient's house, steps over the heart attack patient, goes to his refrigerator, opens it up, and says, "I have to take out all the fatty foods in the refrigerator." Meanwhile the guy's dying of a heart attack.

So that was the idea—with the TARP, what you were going to do with the TARP is use this money to buy dodgy assets out of the banking system. That's not a bad idea: Ultimately, this heart attack patient, you're going to have to take the crap out of his refrigerator. But first you have to restart his heart! And in the end they realized this. The Fed started a program of buying commercial paper directly to get the short-term credit market moving again; the government instituted some FDIC guarantee programs for money-market funds and for guaranteeing bank issuance.

The other thing that needed to be done was recapitalization of the banks. And that, I think, probably does need to happen before you start buying assets out of the banks, but again, it's not something you do before you restart short-term credit.

So these are all pieces of the puzzle, but they kind of did them all in the wrong order.

**n+1:** You were saying last time that they'd injected liquidity into the banks, and the banks gave it right back to the Fed. So that's a failed policy.

**HFM:** Well, come on, you can't expect—what's that old saying, where Kissinger asked Chou En-Lai, "What do you think of the French Revolution?" and he said, "It's too early to tell." The thing is, this policy is new, and it's going to take some time for the banks to start lending again. They will start lending again. We are seeing evidence of the credit markets unfreezing. In the first week of the year, there were a number of very large bond issues, for the first time in a long time. Again, top-quality corporates—GE Capital, McDonald's—top-quality sovereigns, Mexico, Brazil. But there was demand for those bonds. That would not have happened in November or early December. So there's a thaw happening; but it takes some for recapitalization to translate into lending. So I wouldn't say it's a failed policy, yet.*

**n+1:** You're saying in November, if McDonald's had said, "I'm going to issue a bond," no one would have bought it?

**HFM:** Not at levels that would have been attractive to them, and not

---

* Bank lending remains stagnant as of early October 2009. The Fed reports total loans and leases held by U.S. commercial banks at $6.77 trillion, down from a peak of $7.3 trillion in October 2008. On the other hand, corporate bond issuance has bounced back vigorously, starting at around the time of this interview. Quarterly issuance dropped as low as $90 billion in the third quarter of 2008 but rebounded to $497 billion in the first quarter of 2009. First-half 2009 total issuance came to $916 billion, a huge jump over the $575 billion issued in the same period of 2008. In fact, the pace of issuance in 2009 represents the fastest on record. It appears one of the consequences of the financial crisis has been the disintermediation of banks in the corporate credit market (www.sifma.org/research/research.aspx?ID=10806). With banks continuing to contract their loan books, companies in need of capital have been forced to make an end run around the banking system and sell bonds to the public. This is not without consequences; for one thing, bond debt tends to be more expensive for borrowers than bank debt. That corporates have managed to issue bonds in such large volumes suggests that the drop in bank lending is not merely a consequence of a generalized rise in risk aversion. Bond buyers are taking plenty of risk. Rather, it supports the idea that the banking system has suffered structural damage, the consequences of which will linger longer than the psychological symptoms of crisis.

at the size they were able to do it at the beginning of January. So it really does feel like the heart attack phase of this is over. Now what we're seeing is the effect of the heart attack on the rest of the body, in the real economy—the layoffs, GDP shrinkage, trade shrinkage, unemployment. All consequences of that heart attack.

**n+1:** What about the thing that started all this—the homeowners, the people who are behind on their mortgages? The foreclosures?

**HFM:** That needs to be part of the solution, but that is something so granular that there's no way it would make sense for the TARP to put that first. How long would it take to solve that problem? It's going to require dealing with hundreds of thousands of households. There's no simple solution. It's not like Congress passes a formula that says, "Take the mortgage and, like, do this formula based on the size of the property and the person's income," and it spits out a new mortgage balance and a new rate and everything's fine. Because every one of these mortgages is a little bit different, the circumstances of the people involved are a little bit different, and the evidence for that is that the loan modifications that have been done to date, if you look at the data for how those loans have fared, the percentage that's gone back into delinquency is incredibly high, like in the high-30s. Why? They might have not been reducing the balance enough; maybe the way the loan has been restructured doesn't provide sufficient relief. Or it could be that this person *never should have been in a house in the first place.*

So modification is something where you're going to have to build a huge infrastructure of people to do this. You're going to need people to go out and meet with these borrowers, and appraisers to go and see what the value of the house really is. Even if you had a formula, an input of that formula is going to be the value of the house, and you can't get the value of the house without someone going and appraising it.

**n+1:** What about that website?

**HFM:** Zillow? Please. If our loan modification process relies on Zillow . . . I think we have a real problem.

+++

**n+1:** So you're not taking the Treasury or Fed jobs. Is there a job you'd take?

**HFM:** Being a regulator would be interesting, and it would be useful to have a lot more financial talent at the SEC. The SEC is an organization of lawyers—they understand the law very well—but they're at a loss when it comes to understanding actual market behavior. The Madoff thing is a pretty good example. The SEC went and looked at Madoff Securities [in 2003], and a lot of people have been very critical of the woman at the New York office who was responsible for that investigation, Meaghan Cheung, and, you know, she had a good educational pedigree, and a good law degree, and I'm sure she knew the securities laws back and forth, but what was needed there was not someone who understood the securities laws, it was somebody who really understood how brokerages work, how asset managers work, how the whole fund of fund system works, and would know the right people to talk to, the right questions to ask, and who would really know if there was a fraud going on. Not a technical violation of the laws, but an actual fraud.

**n+1:** What would you do at the SEC?

**HFM:** There's people out there—I've dealt with them—I know that they're doing things wrong, I know they're committing crimes. I would love to show up in their office with a badge: "Payback time!"

**n+1:** What sort of thing do you mean?

**HFM:** The idea of the Chinese walls that people talk about in broker-dealers, in investment banks, is a joke. This is supposed to be the separation between the investment bankers and trading—in other words, that traders shouldn't be able to take advantage of information that the institution derives from its advisory activities. It's not a Chinese wall, it's a Chinese screen door—this is *obvious*. And yet the SEC doesn't seem to be all over that.

**n+1:** You would go into a bank and say, "You people aren't using the wall"?

**HFM:** "You don't have a Chinese wall! You have a screen door!" Also there's the peddling of sometimes dangerous derivatives. People should be able to trade whatever they want, within reason, but there needs to be proper risk disclosure, and anybody who has been on the buy side and has had structured products peddled to them knows the kind of tricks that are used to sell them, and knows that there are serious flaws in risk disclosure, serious flaws in the way things get sold, and then you see the consequences of this: They're really dire. A good example of this is some currency "hedges" that were sold recently to corporates in Brazil and Mexico. Maybe this wouldn't be under the SEC's purview, but that blew up some big, established companies in both of these countries. In the last week, one of the big Brazilian meatpackers had to file for bankruptcy because it was sold some alleged currency hedges by U.S. banks that actually *created* a ton of risk. They were totally speculative.

In Mexico, Commerci, which is like a Walmart competitor, a big established company, basically went bust because they were sold these structured currency hedges that blew up in their face. I'd *love* to go to these banks and say, "You're selling derivatives to corporates. Show me how you're doing that." The muni market, the way that municipalities are taken advantage of when they issue debt—they issue debt, and the investment bank says, "Well, you should do an interest rate swap along with that," and they just get utterly raped on the interest rate swap. I'd love to go in and see how that stuff is priced and how it's marketed to these municipalities, who by necessity, by definition, are going to be a lot less sophisticated than the investment bank.

**n+1:** You're saying American investment banks did this in Brazil and Mexico?

**HFM:** Yeah.

**n+1:** And the Brazilians were like, "Oh, it's American investment banks, they wouldn't cheat us"?

**HFM:** Well, the salesperson was probably Brazilian, at the Brazilian office of an American investment bank, but yeah, the treasurer or CFO of that company is taken out by the salesperson down there and persuaded that this is a really great way to enhance revenue and hedge at the same time, and, "Yeah, if there's a very big move in the currency, the risk multiplies, but don't worry, that's not going to happen." I mean, I'd love to hear how that stuff is getting sold.

And that caused *real damage* in Brazil and Mexico. The SEC tends to be focused on stuff that's a lot more technical. They're very focused on technical violations of insider trading laws. And, you know, what are the consequences of insider trading? I don't know. If people believe the market is rigged, then people aren't going to trade in the market, okay, but the kinds of violations that they go after are not going to cause the same magnitude of damage as selling really risky derivatives to a company to the point where you could blow up that company. I mean, that's just much more disruptive. But it's not as clear a violation of the rules as, "Okay, Joe Schmo had material nonpublic information about company X, because he was on the restructuring committee, and then he decided to sell his bonds. Even though maybe that information didn't have a meaningful effect on the price, technically it's material nonpublic information, and we are going to punish that guy." It seems to me they're focused on the wrong things. Not because they're bad people or because they're not intelligent people, but because if you're a lawyer, that's how you think.

+ + +

**n+1:** So the Madoff thing—what was interesting about that?

**HFM:** The Madoff thing was incredible. What was incredible was that it was one of these situations where kind of everybody knew except the people who needed to know. When the news came across the tape here, the trading day was over, and there weren't that many people in the office. It said: "Bernie Madoff arrested." I had never heard of Bernie Madoff, okay? But one of the guys here who is very active in the options world, which is what Bernie Madoff was allegedly trading, as soon as the headline came across—it didn't say what he was arrested for—he said two things. He said, "I knew it, I knew that guy was a fraud." And the second thing he said was, "This is going to be huge. This is going to be the biggest thing ever." So here is a guy who happens to trade options in our office—just seeing the words "Bernie Madoff arrested," he knew exactly what had happened.

So I immediately went to the guy in our office who does the black box trading. Because what Bernie Madoff did, it sounded to me a little bit like black box trading, and I said to him, "Gosh, Bernie Madoff was arrested. If it turns out that his book needs to be unwound tomorrow, is this going to cause big disruptions in our market? Should we

just turn off our machine?" And that guy, he had also heard of Bernie
Madoff, and he said, "No, no, of course not." I'm like, "Why?" He's
like, "He doesn't have any book. It was all a Ponzi scheme, I'm sure of
it." So these people had known forever, it was something that people
*in that world* knew—they heard about his returns, and they said,
"There's just no way that anybody has returns that stable." Doing the
strategy that he alleges he was doing, which was what he calls split-
strike conversion—which is basically you are buying stock, and selling
calls, and buying puts, so it's sort of like you're buying stock and your
downside is limited by options and your upside is limited by options—
it's quite easy to simulate it, and you can tell that there's no way that if
you just did that mechanically, you could generate the returns that he
generated. Of course, to be fair to the people who fell for it, he didn't
say he was doing this all the time. He said, "Sometimes I'm in the
market, sometimes I'm out of the market." His market timing could
be the source of the returns. But everybody who's a professional investor knows there's *no way* that somebody would have over that period
of time such good market-timing ability that he could generate the
stability of returns that he did.

So it was quite obvious to professionals that this guy was a fraud.
But the source of the fraud, there was some disagreement. Some
people said, "Oh, it's just a Ponzi scheme." Other people said, "No, it's
not a Ponzi scheme. Bernie Madoff also runs a market-making opera-
tion." Which means, if you or I put an order at Fidelity to buy stock,
Fidelity routes that order to a market maker. Bernie Madoff was one of
those market makers—he paid for order flows, so he saw people's order
flows. One thing you worry about with a market maker is that the market maker will use the information about customer order flow to trade
in front of the customers. So, for example, if I say, "I'd like to buy one
hundred shares of IBM at 100," and the market maker gets that order,
he knows I'm not going to withdraw that order, I'm just leaving that
order out there all day; he effectively has an option to sell IBM at 100,
because he can just fill my order. So what he does—illegally—is he

goes out there and he buys IBM at, you know, 100 spot 01, and he just waits and hopes that it goes up. If it goes up to 103, he sells it, and then he tells me, "Sorry, your order didn't get filled." If, in fact, something bad happens, and IBM trades down to 98, he just fills my order at 100. So he has no downside.

That's illegal; that's known as front-running. So some people thought that that's what Bernie Madoff was really doing, that's how he generated these returns, it was by front-running. And that's sort of plausible, that you could make the kinds of returns that he made if you committed that particular illegal act. But not on $50 *billion of capital.* You could make those kinds of returns on some small amount of money, or some amount of money that's proportional to the order flow you're seeing, but he wasn't seeing tons and tons of order flow.

So it was like an open secret, and yet he was still able to raise all this money and evade the scrutiny of the regulators. It was pretty amazing.

**n+1:** And when we say it's been huge, what does that mean exactly?

**HFM:** In other words, the magnitude of the losses would be enormous. It's funny: The implications for the financial markets are surprisingly small, given the size of the fraud, because there were no stocks, there were no positions, there's nothing to liquidate—there was nothing there. But there are longer-term implications for the hedge fund world, because the way that he raised a lot of his money was through funds-of-funds. And many hedge funds, their biggest investors are funds-of-funds. And I think the funds-of-funds model has been very seriously damaged by the Madoff affair. These funds-of-funds charge fees, and the value proposition they offer to investors is, "Look, you're not a professional investor, you don't want to spend all your time figuring out which hedge fund to invest in and monitoring them. We do all that for you. We do tons of due diligence, we separate the real investors from the flimflam artists, and we make sure that you're only invested in the best hedge funds." Some very high-profile funds-of-funds got stung by Madoff. Now, does it mean that they don't do any due diligence? Well, clearly there are some funds-of-funds out there that are pure marketing organizations, and they just have some suave, well-connected people who are able to inspire confidence among the wealthy and separate them from their assets. But many funds-of-funds that do have real due diligence still got stung by Madoff. And it makes people question the value proposition: "If a number of funds-of-funds were stung by Madoff, what are these funds-of-funds really doing? Forget it, I'm pulling my money from funds-of-funds." And if that happens, then the funds-of-funds have to pull their money from hedge funds, who had nothing to do with Madoff—Madoff wasn't even really a hedge fund; the structure that he used, managed accounts, is not even a hedge fund—then it has implications for hedge funds, because a big source of capital for hedge funds is damaged reputationally.

Now, clearly anybody who invested, it was a due diligence failure of some magnitude or another. But it was probably apparent to a number of them that there was no way Madoff could have generated the returns that he said he was generating merely by doing split-strike conversion. And this gets to the point that you cannot cheat an honest man. They probably believed that really what was going on was that he was front-running his order flow. He couldn't tell you that, but the funds-of-funds must have thought, "Yeah . . . he's really generating these returns, not the way he says he is, but I can figure out how he is, and I understand, given what he's doing, that he can't really talk about it, but I'm still going to invest, because I want to be part of that scam." And that's, in its own way, disappointing.

**n+1:** When you went to the guy with the black box, was he sitting on the black box? Was he— [*starts laughing*]

**HFM:** I told you, the black box is gray and it's off-site!

**n+1:** Okay. He wasn't riding— [*dissolves into helpless laughter*] I'm sorry.

**HFM:** He wasn't in the box, on the box, astride the box, athwart the box.

**n+1:** He was just sitting at his computer, like everybody else.

**HFM:** He was sitting at his computer like everybody else, and that computer was connected to the box . . .

**n+1:** All right, all right.

**HFM:** By a series of tubes!

+ + +

**n+1:** So next week Obama is inaugurated—are you—

**HFM:** Am I going? No, I'm not going.

**n+1:** Okay, well, what do you think of the new New Deal, and what are you worried about?

**HFM:** Well, look, first of all, I wasn't an Obama supporter, but I've been very impressed with the appointments that he's made, I have to give him credit: He's recruited a very solid economic team, and that's reassuring.

What do I fear? The stimulus package scares me a little bit. Not because I think the stimulus is a bad idea—I think the stimulus is a good idea—but I fear it will be executed in a way that will be ineffective as stimulus but creates a lot of problems down the road. Ultimately what you're looking for in a stimulus is, you're saying, "There's a shortfall of demand right now, there's a shortfall of aggregate demand relative to aggregate supply. So we need to stimulate demand." What you want to do is find things that the government can spend on today that will soak up some of that excess aggregate supply and that down the road will either yield returns to help pay back the debt that's being taken on or will obviate spending down the road. So an example would be, "Let's take all the bridge maintenance that needs to be done in the next five years, and let's just do it all in the next two years. Right? By the time that's done, hopefully the economy will be growing again, and then we don't have to spend the money that we would have had to spend then." Or if schools are overcrowded, "Let's give aid to municipalities that need to build more schools. They're going to have to do it at some point; let's just do it now. All of the construction workers who aren't working on housing, they can go work on building schools, and, you know, in a year or two when the economy's recovering, all the school building that we need to do in the next few years is done, and, you know, they can go back to building housing." I think that's ideally what you want to do with stimulus.

What I fear is that stimulus is just going to mean spending. It's going to mean creating programs that create permanent spending requirements, and that's going to be a real problem, because the amount of stimulus that's being proposed, it's *so much money*, we can't spend at that level permanently. We're borrowing, and ultimately spending will probably have to be lower than it would have otherwise been, in order to pay back that borrowing. Or you're going to wind up with serious damage to the creditworthiness of the U.S. So that worries me.

We've had the government intervene in a lot of unusual ways, or a lot of unwonted ways, to try and solve the crisis. And ultimately many of those ways are about the government assuming risk onto itself to relieve the private sector of risk. And the government can say, "You know what, we're going to guarantee bank deposits," and people are calm because they view the government as a good credit in a way that they didn't view banks as a good credit. But there's a point at which the government takes so much risk onto itself that its credibility is eroded. We've seen that in some other countries—actually, what's happening in Ireland is a good example of that. Ireland basically guaranteed all bank liabilities, and suddenly Irish sovereign credit is very damaged, and credit protection on Ireland, which was once considered one of the best credits in the EU, now it costs about 2.5 percent a year to guarantee against default. We don't want to get to that point in the U.S.

**n+1:** But weren't you saying that that is specifically something that can't happen, really, to the U.S.?

**HFM:** Well, no: if the government is feckless enough it could happen. Maybe it would be reflected not in credit spreads but in expectations of inflation. The U.S. would inflate rather than default, but those are both bad outcomes. There's this professor at Princeton named Edward Tenner, he writes a lot about safety technology, and he says that a lot of safety technology, it doesn't actually make things safer; it's about trading off catastrophic risks against chronic risks. He uses the example of rigid molded ski boots. Before you had these boots, if you had a problem, the problem was rare, but you broke your leg or ankle catastrophically. With modern boots, people very rarely break their legs anymore, but they more frequently wind up with knee ligament damage, so it's a chronic problem. I think when you're talking about government intervention, it's kind of in the other direction: It's more broadly about trading off rare and catastrophic risks against chronic risks. So if a higher-than-usual unemployment and slow economy is something like a chronic risk, the government can deal with that by borrowing and spending on stimulus. If the government takes all this risk onto itself, it may attenuate those chronic risks, but at the risk of you might get to the point where something goes wrong in the U.S. and then the government's creditworthiness is in jeopardy and you have a *huge* mess. It's like building floodwalls on a river: You could have a little bit of flood every year, you build floodwalls so you don't, but every fifty years you have a flood that's bigger than the floodwall, the floodwall collapses, and it's just catastrophic. You have the same issue with the government. We have to be careful, because the government's capacity to absorb risk is not infinite. Its perceived creditworthiness is not infinite. The stimulus is enormous. If it's spent properly, in a way that people see will yield dividends or will obviate spending somewhere down the road, then I think it's perfect. But if it's permanently altering the fiscal landscape in a way that makes the country less creditworthy, that would be bad. And that worries me.

And I'm sure Obama and his team understand that, but he's not the only guy in the room—there's Congress, and Congress has different priorities, and may wish to spend on things that don't really make a lot of sense.

**n+1:** When you're talking about this catastrophic scenario, what would that actually look like?

**HFM:** It could be a creditworthiness issue—one of the ratings agencies could downgrade the U.S. from its triple-A rating.

**n+1:** And then what happens?

**HFM:** Think about what happened in October, but with no party that's creditworthy enough to be able to step in and soothe people's fears. It would be like October times ten. Bank runs, and the government unable to issue a guarantee that would be convincing to people. Or it could be that people fear inflation and the fear of inflation creates inflationary momentum, and you have a real inflation problem at the same time as the economy is doing poorly. Or it could lead to a dollar crash. Foreigners could think, "Gosh, there's no more perfect credit in the U.S. anymore. I don't want dollars. I want to get out of dollars."

**n+1:** What happens if the dollar crashes?

**HFM:** Our standard of living goes down. We can afford fewer imported goods, we have inflation at the same time as the economy is maybe contracting or doing poorly, which is not a pleasant thing. It would have big distributional consequences—generally inflation hits the poor harder because they have fewer ways to hedge against it, to cope with it—and it could really stress our political system.

**n+1:** So a pair of sneakers costs $500?

**HFM:** I don't think we'd have hyperinflation. Think about the late seventies, that kind of inflation and that kind of economic outlook. It would lead to a longer recession, in the long term a lower standard of living.

**n+1:** Wait, wait, aren't we already in a worse situation than the late seventies?

**HFM:** We don't have an inflation problem like the late seventies. We don't have unemployment yet like the late seventies.* So we're not there yet. We might get there. It might look like an emerging-markets crisis. What the U.S. has always had—it's not just the lender of last resort, it's the borrower of last resort. The sovereign credit of the U.S. has always been unquestioned. And that's a really powerful tool. If you lose that tool, you lose a lot of policy options. And that means that whatever challenges we have to face are going to be really amplified.

I don't think that's likely, but we run a higher risk of that if the stimulus program actually creates permanent spending commitments instead of truly being a stimulus.

---

* Unemployment actually peaked in November 1982 at 10.8 percent. (By comparison, estimated unemployment in 1933 was closer to 25 percent.) At the time of this interview, the unemployment rate was 7.2 percent. As of November 2009, it has reached 10.2 percent.

**n+1:** Are you worried about the fact that the Chinese own all this debt?

**HFM:** No. I think it'd be better, obviously, if we didn't have the kinds of external imbalances that we face, that we've had in the past, obviously it'd be better if we came into this crisis with a more balanced current account. But I think the Chinese, it's as much their problem as it is our problem—they're the ones holding trillions of dollars of our paper, so we're kind of lashed together in a way.

**n+1:** You know, we talk, and you tell me all the bad stuff that's happening, but you're relatively optimistic, and then there's all this objectively bad stuff that's happening . . . but I just can't—I just have trouble picturing it.

**HFM:** Trouble picturing what? How we're going to get out of this?

**n+1:** No, I have trouble picturing what it's going to look like when we're *in it*. Because we're not quite in it yet, right?

**HFM:** Yeah, we're not quite in it yet, but we're getting there. The financial sector led this crisis, and you're only seeing the effects on the real economy now. We've seen the distress of the real estate market in certain parts of the country. We know what that looks like: a high level of foreclosures, a lot of new developments that never got sold, that kind of fall apart, that are just sitting there or are half built and get abandoned. It leads to a lot of unemployment; we see that in the construction industry in a lot of these regions. I think it's attenuated by the fact that a lot of labor in the construction industry in those regions was illegal, so it's not as palpable to the rest of us, and some of them go home, and the rest of them are a little bit invisible. But what we're going to see is—it's going to look like—well, were you in

New York after the dot-com bubble popped? You had a lot of friends who were out of work; the restaurants were kind of empty. Just imagine that, but it's happening everywhere. And not just in particular industries. And not for a short period of time but for a fairly long period of time.

# AFTERMATH

As the shock wears off in the late winter, people begin to look around and ask what happened. Early in 2009, Andrew Cuomo, the New York state attorney general, begins investigating year-end executive pay packages as well as asking questions about the Bank of America takeover of Merrill at a share price far higher than Merrill's dismal performance would have indicated. (It eventually emerges that Bank of America chairman Ken Lewis allowed himself to be strong-armed into the move by Paulson and Bernanke.) Cuomo also investigates the less shocking year-end bonuses at AIG, then testifies to Congress about them. Congress holds a series of hearings in which they berate AIG executives for handing out lavish bonuses and attending a fancy company retreat even as the company received an $85 billion federal bailout. "They were getting manicures, facials, pedicures, and massages while American people were footing the bill," says Representative Elijah Cummings (D-Md.). "And they spent another $10,000 for, I don't know what this is, leisure dining. Bars?"

January 25: The New York Times *reports that disgraced Lehman Brothers CEO Richard Fuld has sold his $13 million house in Florida to his wife for ten dollars, apparently to protect it from potential lawsuits and creditors. "Housing prices are falling around the country," comments the* Times, *"but this one sounds hard to believe."*

In early February, President Obama's selection for Health and Human Services Secretary, Tom Daschle, withdraws his nomination because of a scandal over the now very delicate matter of unpaid taxes.

In mid-February, the California legislature fails to pass its budget, "casting doubt," according to one report, "on Gov. Arnold Schwarzenegger's ability to prevent the nation's most populous state from sinking into the abyss."

*At the end of February, rumors swirl that Citi needs more government support and may end up nationalized. On February 27, the government converts Citi's preferred shares into common equity and ends up owning a third of the bank.*

*Hit by falling advertising revenue, the* Rocky Mountain News, *the oldest paper in Colorado, closes. The* Seattle Post-Intelligencer *prints its final paper edition and goes online-only. The* New York Times *threatens to close the* Boston Globe. *Hearst threatens to close the* San Francisco Chronicle. *The* Times *fires a hundred employees after promising no layoffs in 2009.*

*In mid-March the Connecticut Working Families Party organizes a bus tour of the homes of AIG executives in Fairfield. "We're going to be peaceful and lawful in everything we do," Jon Green, the director of Connecticut Working Families, tells the* Times. *"I know there's a lot of anger and a lot of rage about what's happened. We're not looking to foment that unnecessarily, but what we want to do is give folks in Bridgeport and Hartford and other parts of Connecticut who are struggling and losing their homes and their jobs and their health insurance an opportunity to see what kind of lifestyle billions of dollars in credit-default swaps can buy."*

*The phrase "populist rage" enters the national vocabulary to describe people who do not want to save Wall Street.*

*On April 12, the Pierre Michel salon on East 57th Street in Manhattan declines to take Ruth Madoff's appointment for her regular foil highlighting, explaining in a statement that serving her might offend some of its other customers. "Color Barrier for Ruth Madoff," reports the* New York Post.

*Meanwhile, the stocks of gun and ammunition manufacturers Smith & Wesson (NASDAQ listing: SWHC), Colt, and Remington see significant gains as gun owners, convinced that Obama is going to infringe on their Second Amendment rights, stock up.*

*HFM travels to China to check on an investment.*

# HFM VI

# POPULIST RAGE

April 15, 2009

Dow: 8,029.62

Liquid Universe Corporate Index Spread over Benchmark: 427

U.S. OTR ten-year: 2.76 percent

Unemployment: 8.9 percent

Foreclosures: 341,180

**n+1:** You were in China.

**HFM:** I was in China, mostly Beijing, a couple of weeks ago, checking on a property investment. The property sector is important: A lot of the pressure on raw materials prices supposedly coming out of China was related to the property sector, to construction. The amount of building that had been going on was enormous and visible, all over Beijing. I saw one luxury housing development after another, most of them just in the process of construction, or recently completed, and . . . sales had last year just come to a halt. It was amazing, the physical reconstruction of that city. A lot of it had to do with the Olympics, but a lot of it also had to do with property speculation.

And Beijing really is not the city that had the most residential property speculation. The optimism that pumped up that sector was pretty incredible. Here you have a provincial city where there was maybe one 4-star hotel—suddenly there are four 5-star hotel projects under construction, and you just wonder who the heck is going to stay in them. A city that really didn't have much in the way of luxury housing suddenly has tons of luxury projects sprouting up, a lot of those getting sold to speculators, with nobody at the end of the chain. Toward the end of last year people realized just how far supply had outrun real demand, and how far prices had run up.

When I visited, it seemed like reality had set in for the developers and they finally started cutting prices. And unlike in the U.S.—it was interesting to see—in the U.S., where prices had run up, I don't think buyers had in their mind a measurement by which they would decide that if prices fell by x percent, property would be fairly valued. But it seemed like in China, people really did have a price target in mind. "I know what rents are, and this is what the rental yield should be, and if prices fall by a certain amount, then I'm ready to buy." And a number of developers just when I was there were cutting prices, and the statistics that came out for February and March showed that there was suddenly a rebound in property sales.* And that's created some optimism about the property sector of China, which spills over into more optimism broadly.

The other thing that's going on in China is that there is a—not unlike in the U.S.—a very concerted effort at fiscal stimulus and a loosening of credit conditions. Lending has really picked up in China. You're starting to see people starting to believe that that's going to lead to China hitting growth targets, maybe even 8 percent this year.† At the same time, you're starting to see the Chinese run down a lot of the inventories of commodities, so they're having to replenish those inventories. People are starting to get optimistic about China, about

---

* By August 2009, according to the National Bureau of Statistics of China, the index of sale prices of buildings in medium-to-large cities had actually increased 2 percent year-on-year.

† As of September 2009, the market consensus forecast for 2009 China GDP growth was 8.3 percent.

the effect of China on the global economy. It's a little bit puzzling . . . China, we talk a lot about it, it's a lot of people. But as an economy, it's still quite small relative to Europe or the U.S. But it looms large in the imagination of the investor class.

**n+1:** Isn't the main issue that they are a manufacturing country?

**HFM:** They're an exporter, and exports have suffered in China. You actually have seen drops in exports, not merely a reduction in the rate of growth, and that's something that would have been inconceivable eighteen months ago. But there's no way that China's going to be a supportive factor to the global economy via exports. The imbalances in the global economy related, to a large extent, to the fact that China was oversaving and therefore was running a very large surplus, the flip side of which was the unsustainable borrowing in the Anglo-sphere economies: the U.S., the U.K., Australia, New Zealand. We were running up current account deficits and borrowing a ton. Those imbalances have to unwind, which means that China's supportive factor is going to be a story about domestic consumption and about domestic investment in China. And so the property sector's a big part of that. It's not about exports; it's about absorption in China, spending in China. If you believe the Keynesian story, that we have suddenly a shortage of demand, well, the place that was underconsuming relative to its potential was the place that built up a trillion dollars of reserves, that had a domestic savings rate in excess of 40 percent. That's China. China needs to consume.

**n+1:** They'll get us out of this thing?

**HFM:** I don't think the Chinese economy is big enough to save the global economy by itself. But if China were to fall into a recession, and Chinese demand were to fall off a cliff, or if the Chinese were to attempt to stimulate their economy by depreciating their currency and try to export their way out of the situation—that would be very damaging to sentiment. And if China manages to grow at 8 percent, and if there is a jump in domestic demand in China, that will have a positive impact at the margin of the global economy. But that effect will be multiplied, in a sense, by the positive effect on sentiment. You know, "Oh gosh, at least there's a source of growth somewhere. China is growing."

**n+1:** What do we mostly buy from the Chinese? We buy T-shirts and sneakers and stuff?

**HFM:** Technology too. And even some semiprocessed goods. The Chinese make a lot of steel. They import steel, but they also export steel. So it's not only low-value stuff anymore: Haier refrigerators and air conditioners, Huawei telephone switching equipment. They're all up and down the value chain; it's not just knickknacks anymore. A lot of things that are built under the American brands. Some of the biggest exporters in China are big multinational companies that are maybe headquartered in the U.S. or Europe and just do a lot of manufacturing there. It's the workshop to the world.

**n+1:** And are there now a lot of Americans and Europeans there with duffel bags selling sneakers and stuff? To even the current account deficit?

**HFM:** No, not yet. It's still Chinese guys saying "Copy watch!" The thing that I always get propositioned for is "Copy watch!" I thought at first it was a watch that makes copies, but in fact it's a knockoff watch. DVDs too. "Copy watch! DVDs!"

**n+1:** Why would they tell you it's a copy watch? I guess they knew you could tell the difference.

**HFM:** Well, they know that you know nobody is going to be selling Rolexes out of a duffel bag on the corner of a street in Beijing. They offer that courtesy out of respect for your intelligence.

+ + +

**n+1:** So the Chinese aren't going to go off the dollar? This is not something we're worried about?

**HFM:** Will the dollar lose its status as a reserve currency? This is an interesting question. I don't believe the dollar will lose its reserve status anytime soon for a variety of reasons. But the reason people overlook is that a lot of reserve buildup is precautionary, not in the sense of being able to buy goods and things if your country has a problem, but in terms of the ability to repay debts that come due if there's a sudden stop of capital flows, and most of the debt outstanding, the international debt outstanding in the world, is denominated in dollars. That's not something you can change overnight. This is debt that's been issued over years and years and years, so if you happen to be indebted in dollars, your economy, the private agents in your economy, not to mention the government, are indebted in dollars, then the monetary authority needs to hoard dollars as a precautionary measure. Hoarding euros isn't necessarily going to help if what you owe is dollars and your goal is to know that your economy can deal with a year-long sudden stop in capital flows. You need to have a reserve, and a composition of reserves, to match up with the composition of your obligations. Most of those are dollars.

Now, if the dollar is to lose its reserve currency status, the first thing you need to see is cross-border borrowing denominated in other currencies. That means the loss of reserve currency status will be a slow process. Why would companies in emerging countries, or governments in emerging countries, seek to borrow in currencies other than dollars over time? Well, that's really where you get into the more standard story about what makes a reserve currency. You're going to borrow in a currency that matches the currency in which most trade flows are denominated, and that means if the U.S. is not a big importer and exporter anymore, well, then maybe people don't denominate their trade flows in dollars anymore. Or if the currency no longer functions as a stable store of value, or people don't want to denominate intertemporal transactions in that currency anymore, and if the dollar were facing, you know, a lot of inflation or the threat of a lot of inflation, or instability in its value, a company isn't going to want to denominate a long-term import contract or export contract in dollars. And so that interferes with the use of the dollar in trade flows, and that will also interfere with the use of the dollar for borrowing and lending.

We don't see that yet. The U.S. is still the biggest economy in the world by a very large margin, and still an enormous exporter/importer. You also need to have a loss of the faith that the currency will have a stable value. And, okay, we might face that if we have a lot of inflation in the U.S. as a result of the mass monetary expansion going on today.

But there needs to be another currency to take its place. With the euro there's a specter that the European Monetary Union could splinter and that could lead to a very unpredictable outcome. Sterling— well, the U.K.'s just not that big of an economy anymore, and the U.K. is embracing unorthodox monetary policy as quickly as we are. The yen—well, seems like the BOJ [Bank of Japan] never really had a strong desire to push the yen as international reserve currency. And the Japanese economy has plenty of problems of its own that can make people wonder about the future value of the yen. And then what? The Chinese? The renminbi isn't even a convertible currency. So that's a nonstarter. The SDR, which is the special drawing right, that's what the Russians and the Chinese have talked about? The SDR isn't really a currency; it's just a unit of account. It's the IMF unit of account: It's really just a basket of dollar, yen, sterling, and euro. I don't think private agents are going to be borrowing and lending in a unit of account that doesn't really exist as a currency by itself.

**n+1:** And so the concern—because last time we talked you outlined a scenario where, you know, the U.S. loses its triple-A rating.

**HFM:** If we continue to rack up debt the way we're racking it up, yes, the U.S. could lose its triple-A rating. But I think that in that scenario, I don't know who—I don't know what major country could be that much better rated than the U.S. Maybe Germany, some small European countries—but they're just not big enough that they would play the same role that the U.S. does, and the euro doesn't belong to any one of those countries. A currency like the euro that is shared among a number of countries that aren't perfectly aligned politically or economically, it's going to be a long time before people feel comfortable enough with the euro that it would represent a big threat to the dollar's reserve currency status.

**n+1:** Because some of the countries in Europe are crazy?

**HFM:** What might happen: The Italians can't adjust their economy to some shock. The way that they used to adjust was by devaluing the lira; now that they're in the euro, if the Italian economy's doing really poorly, they can't devalue. But say the German economy is doing well, and the ECB [European Central Bank] has to deliver the policy for a country that's doing well and a country that's doing poorly, and it chooses to tailor its policy for Germany. There'd be a temptation for Italy to say, "We're going to get out of the euro." Now, that's a very speculative scenario, but it's one that people do talk about. Alternatively, the strongest countries could get fed up with the political pressure from the weaker economies to debase the euro, and you have an exit of the stronger countries from the euro. So in that scenario it's not that a Portugal or an Italy can't take the discipline of the ECB; it's that the ECB is actually undisciplined because the weaker countries wind up getting the upper hand, and you have Germany exiting and reestablishing the deutschmark, reverting to a really hard currency. So if people talk about the possibility of the fracture of the European Monetary Union—and if you look at all the research, there's plenty of talk about that; a lot of it is to debunk the scenario, but if you have to debunk the scenario it means that people are thinking about it—that means it would be very difficult for the euro to take the place of the dollar.

It's also about how ugly an exit would be. That's not something that the treaties that established the European Monetary Union really contemplate.

**n+1:** So it's not that the dollar is so great; it's just that there's nothing else.

**HFM:** It's interesting you say that. Currencies are all about exchange rates; there are two parts to every exchange rate. You can't really think about currencies in absolute terms. You're exchanging them for something, whether it's goods or other currencies. So to say that it's not that the dollar is so great, it's that other currencies have equally serious problems or worse problems—that's the equivalent of saying that the dollar is great.

+ + +

**n+1:** In China, did you sense that there was anger at the U.S.?

**HFM:** I'm dealing mainly with businesspeople who probably aren't going to harangue me. But it was funny. I did sense a little bit of a strain of maybe . . . *triumphalism* is the wrong word, but maybe a little amusement at the U.S.'s predicament. And so definitely at some of the meetings I had—more than one—there were some comments about how it was now China that was going to be helping the U.S. by continuing to lend to it. And the power relations had reversed. There was a little, a sort of . . . call it a gentle raillery.

**n+1:** I was under the impression that the Chinese have been lending to us for a long time?

**HFM:** Definitely. Definitely. But the sense now is that they're lending to us out of a policy decision in order to prevent the U.S. from having serious problems. I don't think that's a fair picture . . . but it's new.

**n+1:** But we've been feeling that way for a while.

**HFM:** That they've been bailing us out? No, that was based on their policy priority to try to stimulate their own economy through exports and keep their currency undervalued, and that required them to lend to us—to get us to buy from them, they had to lend to us. But now they sort of feel like it's not something they're doing for purely selfish reasons; now it's China's responsibility as an important economic power in the world to keep lending to the U.S. so the U.S. doesn't have problems.

**n+1:** And, ah, this is, they find this . . . ?

**HFM:** They think it's funny.

+ + +

**n+1:** Then you returned to the U.S. What did you find?

**HFM:** I found that the sense of total dread and helplessness that had been the atmosphere of the financial markets in December and January and February was really kind of lifting. And there's been a greater sense of optimism and the feeling that perhaps at least the pace of deterioration of the economy has stopped increasing, and so the second derivative has gone flat. You don't need me to tell you, you can see it in the equity market, you can see it in the credit spreads, that there's been a real rebound, and that the apocalypse is no longer priced into the financial markets.

**n+1:** Ah-huh. What about the continued bank bailouts?

**HFM:** That's part of the reason the apocalypse is not priced in anymore—we haven't had any enormous bank failures. And some of the banks have come out and said that their business in January and February and March was profitable—Citi was the first to do it, Bank of America said so, Goldman actually reported this week. Personally, I think it's a load of bollocks. I mean, as a bank, you have a lot of freedom to mark your assets where you please, particularly the loan book. You can show a profit, you can show whatever profit you want. You have a lot of scope to manage your P&L [profit-and-loss statement]. In the emerging markets I've often seen banks showing quarterly profits until the day they go belly-up.

So I don't put a lot of stock in the pronouncements from banks that, "Oh, we made money in January and February, everything's fine." In an environment where we really don't know how bad loan delinquencies are going to get, it's very theoretical to even talk about P&L over a two-month period. You don't really know how much the loans will deteriorate. Where you're marking them is pretty much a guess. It will take a much longer period of time to figure out how much you should provision against those loans. But people have reacted well to those statements because they were pricing in the collapse of one of the big banks.

**n+1:** So if this is all unrealistic, and the banks have just kind of announced in a vague way that they've made money for a couple months, how come this makes people feel good?

**HFM:** If I knew that, I'd probably be a better investor.

**n+1:** You are a great investor!

**HFM:** I would be a more successful investor, because to me, you're right, it's kind of meaningless. But I think animal spirits are very important. You hear bad news and horror stories all day long, you become nervous, you don't want to take risk, and you tend to sell your risky assets. If you start to hear positive chatter, even if a lot of those individual data points, when you dig down, turn out to be not well grounded, it might set your mind at ease. One of the things about investing is you're being bombarded with information all the time, and not every piece of information can you look into closely, so part of what informs your risk tolerance is emotion, and your emotion can very much be affected by random pieces of just headlines and pieces of information that you only process in a very shallow way. And if they all sound sort of positive, that tends to put people at ease and they're willing to take more risk. As an investor, it would be great if I could just be a robot and disregard any information except, you know, information I could be really sure was meaningful, but I'm a human being like every other investor. Other than the black boxes! They're not human.*

**n+1:** It would be better to be a robot?

**HFM:** It would be better to be a robot.

---

* As of October 2009, the IMF was estimating that the U.S. banking system has another $400 billion to provision for. It is kind of a joke, then, to talk about accounting profits. There's $400 billion more of losses to take!

**n+1:** You don't think that Citi is a zombie bank?

**HFM:** Citi's definitely a zombie bank. Of course!

**n+1:** So why do we keep feeding it blood?

**HFM:** I don't know; I think it's foolish.

**n+1:** Because you've said from the start we have to recognize our losses.

**HFM:** At the beginning of this crisis, it was possible that the whole financial system was a wreck. We had a very poor handle on how bad the situation was, where the worst assets were distributed, and there was pretty much blind panic. If you have Citi fail in that situation, I think it would have been hard to control the repercussions. I think now that we have a little better idea which banks are the most problematic, which banks are actually relatively safe—some banks that were maybe on the brink have been strengthened with recapitalization from the government. I think it wouldn't be as catastrophic for a bank like Citibank, not to fail, but to be nationalized and for stakeholders other than shareholders to maybe lose some money. Now, Citibank is an important corporate bank; I don't think you'd want depositors to lose money. But I certainly think it's fair to say that this bank is deep into negative equity, and shareholders need to get zeroed, preferred shareholders and subdebt holders need to get zeroed, and senior debt holders need to take a haircut.

**n+1:** What about the depositors?

**HFM:** I think you would protect the depositors. First of all, retail depositors are all protected by the FDIC. Corporate depositors, I think it would be very disorderly to try to take a bite out of the corporate depositors at Citi. But look, you don't need to look that far. Let's be incremental about it. Why do shareholders—let's start with the common shareholders. Why do the common shareholders still have anything? Let's start with that.

**n+1:** What do you mean?

**HFM:** They've been diluted, but they haven't been zeroed.

**n+1:** Let's zero them!

**HFM:** I agree. Maybe that will happen. Another problem that maybe will come is the time it takes to actually do this. There's sort of a diachronic aspect to this, that if you go and zero the shareholders of Citibank today, then the shareholders of Bank of America say, "Maybe we're next." And then Bank of America can't raise private capital if it needs to, and it creates panic. I think, therefore, that it's wise that the government is quietly going and doing all of these stress tests. Now, I'm not saying that the stress tests they're doing are realistic or valuable, but let's assume for a second that the government were doing very valuable and relevant stress tests.

**n+1:** Wait, what's a stress test?

**HFM:** The stress test is basically an examination of the bank and how robust the bank is to various economic scenarios. They go in and they look at all the assets, and they make some assumptions about how those assets would respond to a very bad recession or high unemployment, and then see whether or not under those circumstances the bank would still be solvent.

**n+1:** So they're not testing their fitness at the bank?

**HFM:** They're not making the bank run on a treadmill. It would actually be funny to watch that; I would love to see Vikram Pandit running on a treadmill.

**n+1:** Okay, they're doing stress tests.

**HFM:** If the government is going to intervene some banks, it should do it very swiftly, and then be able to say that the banks that needed to be intervened have been intervened, and the banks that haven't been intervened, it means that we've taken a look at them and we think they are reasonably healthy. Because otherwise you can create a cascading panic. And that's why the government really did need to prop up banks for a while, in order to be able to get all of the information it needed to figure out which banks were really in trouble, and which banks just needed some temporary support to deal with the panic.

**n+1:** So which banks do you think should be wiped out?

**HFM:** Oh my gosh! It would be highly irresponsible for me to say which banks should be wiped out, because I haven't been able to go and take a look at their books. No, but look, Citi is one that people talk about, is probably the poster child of the big banks. And our bank system has become unfortunately very concentrated. Deconcentrating the banking system is going to be an important project going forward, but right now it's highly concentrated. So what are the banks that matter? The banks that matter are Citibank, Bank of America, Wells Fargo, and JPMorgan Chase. I don't think anyone would say that JP-Morgan Chase has a problem. I don't think there're too many people who would say that Citibank *doesn't* have a problem. And there's a lot of debate about Wells and about Bank of America. You know, Bank of America was perceived as being quite healthy. But then it made some very puzzling acquisitions: Countrywide, which was one of the prime offenders in the subprime crisis, and then Merrill Lynch, that had a huge amount of really toxic waste on its books in the form of mortgage-backed and asset-backed securities. And then Wells: People looked at Wells and thought that Wells was not a bank that was very involved with the securities side of things, but Wells bought Wachovia and together, Wells and Wachovia, they have problems. They are perceived as having problems in their loan books. For example, Wells has an enormous home equity line of credit portfolio, which is all generally second lien. There's a first mortgage in front of most of these loans, and there's a lot of uncertainty as to whether there will be any recovery for those loans if they go bad. And the book is enormous. So people worry about that.

**n+1:** Now the FDIC has raised their insurance to $250,000. Is that for depositors?

**HFM:** Yes. Per account holder per bank. So you can have deposits in many different banks, you're insured for $250,000 per bank.

**n+1:** So why not wipe out everybody's savings over that amount at Citigroup?

**HFM:** Well, I think that, you know, that would just lead to a lot of companies that use Citibank for their treasury function, you know, not being able to make payroll. It would lead to bankruptcies; it would lead to a lot of stories about people who did have more than $250,000, for whatever reason, having their lives ruined. For instance, let's say, not that anybody in this interview has this problem, but let's say when it comes time for your quarterly estimated taxes, you need to pay more than $250,000. I mean, you need to move amounts of money larger than that, you're going to go through the pain in the ass of having three different bank accounts at three different banks? And send three different checks to the Treasury? It would lead to no company, nobody at all, keeping more than $250,000 at a U.S. bank. And I think that would be an inefficient outcome.

**n+1:** Okay, let's pretend that Citigroup is going to be taken over. What is that going to look like?

**HFM:** Well, the government winds up injecting some capital into Citigroup, diluting the shareholders down to zero—that's one scenario. Another scenario is that it goes beyond that, and that you have something that looks a little like a bankruptcy in that Citigroup says that it's not going to pay its preferred shareholders or subordinated debt holders or maybe goes as far as approaching its senior bond holders and saying, "Look, we're not going to be able to pay your bonds on time or in full." And goes through a restructuring process whereby the preferred shareholders and the common shareholders probably get wiped out, and the senior debt holders no longer have debt claims, they become equity holders in the bank.

**n+1:** And does the government come and run the bank?

**HFM:** They'll appoint new top management; there'll be a new board, but it's not like every teller is going to be fired and replaced by someone from the National Guard. Citigroup, there's value to the franchise, and that value should be preserved. So I think Citigroup would still exist, it would still operate, it's just that on the liability side of its balance sheet the claims would be reshuffled. Some claims would be extinguished: Common shareholders, preferred shareholders, subordinated debt holders, probably some of the senior debt holders would lose their senior debt claim and become equity. But Citibank would still operate.*

---

* Vikram Pandit remained CEO of Citigroup as of October 2009, though in January 2009 Dick Parsons replaced Sir Win Bischoff as chairman. The government has generally refrained from taking an activist role as shareholder, preferring to restrict itself to a more wonted regulatory role. For example, Treasury Department "pay czar" (strictly speaking, not a Romanov, but rather a "special master") Kenneth Feinberg must sign off on compensation plans for the top-paid officers.

+ + +

**n+1:** There was an article in the *Atlantic* last month that compared the problems we're dealing with, with the banks and the financial sector, to an emerging market oligarchy where the financial interests are so entrenched and so involved with government that you really need to smash the whole thing.*

**HFM:** I saw that article. The financial sector has too much power, too much say in how the problems in the financial sector should be dealt with. I think there's something to that, although I don't indulge in the more lurid fantasies of how Goldman Sachs orchestrated a hijacking of the government. But I do think the approach of the Bush administration and the Obama administration has been insufficiently tough with the financial sector. And let me be clear: Not being sufficiently tough isn't a question of calling back some guy's bonus at AIG, which is just a total sideshow, or saying that management can only be paid $x$ dollars. I mean, that's not real toughness, that's purely symbolic and kind of pointless and maybe even destructive. I mean toughness in the sense of saying, "There are certain institutions that need to be shot or nationalized or rapidly downsized," or institutions where losses need to be distributed to the point where shareholders are wiped out, and even other parts of the capital structure are forced to endure permanent losses.

**n+1:** Why have they failed to be tough in this way? Because they're friendly with those people?

**HFM:** No, I think they feared the consequences of that for confidence, and that might have been the right call early on in the crisis, when there was too much uncertainty. But I think now that we've got the

---

* Simon Johnson, "The Quiet Coup," *The Atlantic*, May 2009.

important things stabilized, and you can do that, why hasn't the government done that yet? Perhaps the people responsible for this policy come from the financial sector, are very close with people in the financial sector—and that's not to say there's a nefarious influence, but the way they think doesn't admit of a world where Citibank gets nationalized. It's just so inconceivable to them that they say, "You just can't do that! It'll cause all of these horrible problems." Well, that was true when the economy was in an extremely unstable state and risk aversion was extreme and panic was abroad in the land. But now I don't think that's the case, and your lack of imagination is not a good grounds for a policy judgment.

**n+1:** But you're from the financial—

**HFM:** I'm from a hedge fund! I never worked in a bank. I think if you talk to people in the hedge fund world, you find probably more people than you might expect would agree with my view that the bailout plan, at least for right now, has been too soft on the banks.

**n+1:** When people always talk about how smart everybody at Goldman is, what do you think about that?

**HFM:** The people that I know there are very smart. The human capital there is a cut above some of the other banks out there. I think that's true.

**n+1:** But surely if they were really smart they'd be working at a hedge fund?

**HFM:** You could make plenty of money at Goldman. And a lot of people at Goldman did leave to start hedge funds, and many of the very successful hedge funds out there are run by Goldman alums. As well as our government.

+ + +

**n+1:** When you were talking about misallocation of resources, right, what you were really talking about was that somebody was given money to do something that didn't need to be done . . .

**HFM:** Exactly. Some very smart, intelligent people, very intelligent physicists, spent their time creating mortgage-backed securities to fool S&P into giving them a rating that they shouldn't have given them. That's one example. Another example is a Mexican, a rural Mexican, swam across the Rio Grande to hammer together houses in the exurbs of Arizona that no one is ever going to occupy.

**n+1:** But somebody . . . money changed hands. And the people who got that money—the misallocatees, say—well, they get to keep it.

**HFM:** Ah, yes, but here's the question: Who paid that Mexican guy to hammer together those houses? Well, the developer. Where did the developer get the money from? The developer got the money from a bank. Where did the bank get the money from? The bank got the money from a depositor. The depositor doesn't think he spent the money. The depositor still thinks he has a claim on the money, right? The problem is that what underlies that claim is an empty, uninhabited, uninhabitable house in Arizona. That's what I mean by allocating the losses. There's a loss there; the depositor doesn't know that he's lost yet.

**n+1:** But he lost that money *to* someone. What I'm saying is, somebody has that money.

**HFM:** Yeah, the Mexican guy who hammered the house; he sent it back to his family in Mexico.

**n+1:** You're saying the Mexican guy has the money? Surely the developer has some of the money?

**HFM:** No! The developer spent it all developing these houses! The developer's bust too.

**n+1:** You're saying the Mexican guy spent all the money? That doesn't make sense.

**HFM:** He spent it on himself, or he sent it to his family, and his family bought stuff they wouldn't have been able to afford otherwise.

**n+1:** Billions of dollars? You're saying the Mexican guy took billions of dollars?

**HFM:** Well, a billion Mexicans . . . not one Mexican guy! How about all the mortgage brokers who were brokering these mortgages that didn't make any sense? They all got paid, right?

**n+1:** Right, those guys! So it's not just—

**HFM:** No! Anybody who worked in sectors where there was a tremendous amount of activity where there shouldn't have been. So we're talking about housing. It means the Mexican guy who hammered together the house. It means the logger who cut down the wood that was used in the structural lumber. The guy who worked at the sawmill. It means the steel company that created the steel for the nails. It means the mortgage broker who sold the mortgage. It means the physicists who decided instead of doing physics they should work on Wall Street to create the asset-backed security that helped to fund the mortgages that the mortgage broker was originating. All of these people were doing things that turned out not to be productive.

The loser was whoever turned out to be the investor at the end of the chain. So there's a loss that needs to be allocated. That's backward-looking. On a forward-looking basis, now we all know there shouldn't be 50 zillion mortgage brokers, right? There shouldn't be 50 zillion people working on this stuff. What do you do with those people now? They need to find—we need to, the economy needs to find—another use for them. These pay scales will shift, and those people will be moved to their highest and best use, right? But the dynamics are very tricky because these are quantities in a—ultimately people are not quantities in an equation, but it's difficult for that mortgage broker to find the right job for himself. Maybe he needs to move across the country. All of that is a slow process. And a costly process. And a difficult and disruptive process.*

**n+1:** Well, but also I mean there might not be jobs for those people.

**HFM:** At some price there'll be jobs for those people. If you have perfectly flexible prices, there will be a clearing price for the labor of people with various skill sets. But yes, they overinvested in skills that maybe aren't worth that much. So if you really know a lot about mortgage brokering, that may be worth nothing. Maybe the only thing you have to offer is the strength of your back when you're moving boxes. And that is a very painful adjustment for somebody to make. I mean, let's just say that we have a class of people who were very highly paid to be witch doctors, and then tomorrow Western medicine comes to the economy, and everybody realizes that witch doctors . . . it's much better to take pills than go to the witch doctors. Well, these witch doctors had some very specific knowledge that was worth a lot but now is worth nothing. But there's some use for them, right? They can become manual laborers. That's a very

---

* There is evidence that the process is under way. The Center for Immigration Studies estimates that the population of illegal aliens in the United States declined from 12.5 million in the second quarter of 2007 to 10.8 million in the second quarter of 2009.

difficult transition. They're not just going to accept that right off the bat, that witch doctor skills are worthless and the price of their labor has gone from very high to practically nothing.

**n+1:** But what I'm saying is, the witch doctors were making a lot of money during this period, and they got to keep that money. Whereas I, me, I didn't make any money. And now they've ruined the economy and I might *never* make any money.

**HFM:** Ah, right, and your point is we should try to get that money back from them?

**n+1:** I don't know. No . . .

**HFM:** They don't have it. They spent it.

**n+1:** No! They couldn't spend all of it.

**HFM:** The mortgage brokers probably spent all of their money. The mortgage-backed securities structurers maybe didn't spend all of their money. But when you have an economy where contracts can be re-written and you can go back and try to claw back money from people years after the fact, that's going to be tremendously destabilizing and it's going to really disincentivize investment in human capital. And it's going to incentivize people to work in the gray economy. I think the answer is, for some of these jobs, jobs like in the investment business, going forth contractually, we should create compensation arrangements where there are clawbacks. But you have to do that by agreement and in advance. You can't reopen contractual arrangements years after the fact. At least not without some strong indications of knowing fraud.*

---

\* As of this writing, only the two Bear Stearns hedge funders Cioffi and Tannin had been indicted. There were numerous other indictments, but those were uncontroversial frauds

**n+1:** Actually, the people who made a lot of money were the people on Wall Street, right?

**HFM:** Well, the physicists who—

**n+1:** Not the physicists! The brokers of this stuff, the sellers of these securities.

**HFM:** Those people made a lot of money, sure.

**n+1:** Okay, those are the people!

**HFM:** Well, I mean, it's one of the things we talked about, that profits and pay, the fraction of profits and pay in the economy that accrued in the financial sector had gone up a lot. And that's going to go back down.

**n+1:** And this goes to a bigger problem. We also talked about these bubbles, right? That they happen and happen, like a wave—it goes from one sector to another sector to a third sector. And then we've had this long bubble in the financial sector. Isn't it possible simply that there was no other place to make money, there was no other place for growth, that people have all the stuff that they need?

**HFM:** Well, look, this is one of the axioms of economics, that people have unlimited wants and limited resources. Personally, I feel like I have enough stuff—it's painful for me when I get a gift. The idea that I have to put it somewhere is painful for me. But then I think if you look at a broad swath of the population of the U.S., and then if you

---

(such as Madoff, Allen Stanford for a Ponzi scheme, Hassan Nemazee for a fraudulent $74 million loan application) or insider trading cases (Raj Rajaratnam and friends). A grand jury apparently was empaneled to see if Joe Cassano, the head of the controversial AIG financial services group, could be indicted, but as of November 2009 it hadn't happened yet. The paucity of indictments is itself worthy of note.

think about poorer countries and people, there's much more that they want. People will always find new things to want.

n+1: But you don't think this is a real, systemic problem we've run into, finally?

HFM: Is it new? Here's what I believe. I believe when you're looking at economies—because I do emerging economies, this is a pretty important part of emerging economies—you have to be epistemologically modest. Let me give you a sort of analogy. When emerging markets were doing well, say in 2005 to 2006, people were saying: "Emerging economies, they've emerged. They've figured out the institutions that are required for sustainable growth."

But Latin America, practically from the time Europeans came to the Western Hemisphere, or very shortly thereafter—North America actually *diverged* from Latin America. There wasn't convergence; there was continued divergence. What are the odds that it just so happens that the day I show up, that the few-year period that I've shown up in the financial markets, that this multi-hundred-year process has suddenly and sustainably reversed? I mean, you have to be incredibly epistemologically immodest to think that. By the same token, we have, you know, ten thousand years of human history where people are always wanting more, making more, and getting more. What's the probability that it just so happens that you and I have been born into the generation where we finally run out of wants? I just think it's impossible. Maybe we're that special—I dream of being special in some way—but I think I'm just another human involved in a very long chain that stretches far back into the past and will stretch far forward into the future, of human beings that have the same intellectual equipment and tend to behave in similar ways.

n+1: You know, we haven't had capitalism for ten thousand years.

**HFM:** But we've had property for ten thousand years. We've had monetary exchange for ten thousand years. We haven't had advanced capitalism, but people have always striven to get more, and in general the trend has been for a higher level of consumption. There've been periods of setback, but the long trend is very clear. I think it's very unlikely that we've suddenly hit our limit, that we can't come up with more needs, and therefore we're at crisis because we can't grow anymore. Ultimately the thing where we might be heading into a change that is challenging to our economies is if, in the advanced economies, we see the end of population growth. And we are seeing some countries where there has been a very important pivot, countries going into long and sustained population shrinkage for reasons not related to war, reasons related to reproductive choices. And it's not clear whether—I take your point that it's not clear whether our brand of capitalism, call it our political economy, capitalism plus the welfare state, can be easily sustained in this era of shrinking population. But that's a much bigger question, and I think it's different from the one you asked.

+ + +

**n+1:** And yet . . .

**HFM:** Yes, I'm taking a semi-sabbatical.

**n+1:** How come?

**HFM:** I'm very burned out. I've been doing this for a very long time. I've taken about, in the last ten years, two vacations that were one week long. All my other time off has been a day here, a day there. So I'm a little burned out. I also think the last eighteen months have been a very stressful time to be in the financial markets . . . just dealing with many more extreme events, which lead to extreme behavior from our counterparties. Behavior that I would've considered surprisingly unethical in the past.

**n+1:** What sort of behavior?

**HFM:** We deal with borrowers who are just taking advantage of the chaos to not pay their debts or steal company money, stuff like that. That is very frustrating. And then, look, I see what's happening to the tax system, and the incentive to work, to continue to do a very stressful job, is declining. I've accumulated a decent amount of wealth, so the return on any given amount of compensation just goes down because of that. Obviously the tax situation in the hedge fund industry is changing a little bit; taxes in New York state have gone up by a significant amount. And federal taxes are going up. It just kind of reaches a point where it's just not worth the aggravation anymore.

**n+1:** So you're the person that nobody thinks exists, who actually works less because of taxes.

**HFM:** It's a factor on the margin, let's say. If I weren't completely burned out, maybe I'd say, "Ah, taxes are a little higher, maybe I'll move to Florida or I'll move to Texas or I'll move to Nevada to lower my tax rate." But I think if you combine the taxes with the fact that I've been under a lot of stress, I've been doing this for a long time, I have a higher amount of wealth, and so on—and the fact that everybody hates people in finance, it's almost embarrassing to say that you work for a hedge fund—when you put all that together, I think it's time to take a step back and reevaluate. So I'm still going to be doing this, but I'm just doing it at a lower intensity for the next couple of months.

**n+1:** So when you talk about the unethical stuff, in what sense are you dealing with these people?

**HFM:** They're our counterparties. They're people we trade with sometimes, companies that we own shares in; sometimes it's companies we own bonds of, sometimes it's companies that we've lent money to. They're behaving in ways that are more sharp-elbowed, just more difficult to deal with. There's more what I consider to be fraudulent behavior. Because one of the things that constrains borrower behavior, particularly in emerging markets, where legal recourse is imperfect, is the idea that they'd like to be able to borrow in the future. But when you get into a credit crunch, the prospect of being able to borrow again anytime soon at a reasonable rate, no matter how well you behave, is very uncertain. So that incentive for good behavior disappears.

**n+1:** And this has been going on in the past . . . six months now?

**HFM:** I'd even say the past year.

**n+1:** And these are people you would not have expected this from?

**HFM:** Well, some of them I would have expected it [from], and, you know, it's just turned out that the circumstances where that behavior surfaces have come about, and it was something I knew I might have to cope with, and I cope with it. Still it's not fun, and sometimes it's unexpected.

**n+1:** So to cope with it, does this mean you have to hire lawyers?

**HFM:** Yes, it's hiring lawyers, it's coming up with nonjudicial ways of putting pressure on people. It's just a lot of arguing on the phone. It's a very different business than making decisions about capital allocation, about trading, right? It's a very different kind of business. It's one that you always have to do a little bit of, but having to do a lot of it all at once, it's very stressful.

**n+1:** Has this been taking up half your time?

**HFM:** Probably around 40 percent.

**n+1:** And even more of your head space, probably?

**HFM:** Yes. I'd say that everybody has a certain amount of aggravation they can take. And it's a fixed quantity, and more of it's being taken up by this kind of stuff. I think it feels like metal fatigue. Like metal—you can bend it, and it has a certain resiliency for a while, but if you keep bending it back and forth it fatigues, and then it becomes brittle and it cracks. And I feel like I've reached a point of brittleness—of psychological brittleness.

In late April the government announces the bankruptcy of Chrysler. In a bit of populist rage of their own, the company's corporate creditors are upset that their preferred stock is getting just 29 cents on the dollar while factory employees are receiving their full severance packages. Obama gives a forceful speech on the subject, singling out those who have tried to oppose the bankruptcy. "A group of investment firms and hedge funds," he says, "decided to hold out for the prospect of an unjustified taxpayer-funded bailout. They were hoping that everybody else would make sacrifices, and they would have to make none. Some demanded twice the return that other lenders were getting. I don't stand with them. I stand with Chrysler's employees and their families and communities."

Banks report their first-quarter results and several post strong profits. Goldman Sachs reports a day early and handily beats expectations. Meanwhile, the mortgage giants taken over by the government continue to post amazing losses: Fannie Mae reports a $23.2 billion first-quarter loss, and Freddie Mac follows with $9.9 billion.

April is the second month in a row that more than 300,000 homes are foreclosed in the United States. Nevada, Arizona, California, and Florida lead the way.

The next interview takes place on one of HFM's new days off.

# HFM VII

# LIFE AFTER THE CRISIS

May 18, 2009
Dow: 8,504.08
Liquid Universe Corporate Index Spread over Benchmark: 339
U.S. OTR ten-year: 3.23 percent
Unemployment: 9.4 percent
Foreclosures: 342,038

**n+1:** We're sitting in a coffee shop, we're sitting here in the middle of the morning on a Monday, a working Monday—

**HFM:** Isn't it delightful?

**n+1:** How long has this been going on?

**HFM:** I've been working a three-day-a-week schedule, what my firm calls a working sabbatical, for about three weeks now. And that's going to continue until the end of the summer.

**n+1:** How's it going?

**HFM:** I find I spend a lot of time working, just from home.

**n+1:** The BlackBerry is still on the table.

**HFM:** Yeah, it's still there. To the extent that you're still exposed to the markets, you can't really be entirely off on a workday. But when I'm working from home at least I have fewer importunate employees, it's harder for annoying salespeople to find me, and the work that I do I finish more quickly. The idea behind taking this working sabbatical is that it'll help me recharge my batteries a little and allow me to play offense again. It's been a year of playing defense, coping with this crisis, and generally doing my job in a reactive way. That's very wearing. Now all I can think about when I'm presented with a new proposal or investment idea is why I should say no, because in the last year and a half, pretty much any risk that you took, any long risk that you took, went sour.

**n+1:** What do you mean by playing defense?

**HFM:** When you're constantly reacting to the market and trying to mitigate damage that various market events could cause for you. When Lehman blew up it was a week of spending time figuring out what exposures we have, and "Do we need to prepare for the next Lehman? How do we change around our counterparty exposure calls for that? What trades do we need to take off or try to move to another counterparty?" Or when the repo markets started to break down, adjusting your portfolio to be less reliant for funding on the repo market. Trying to be prepared for redemptions from investors. If you get into a mental defensive crouch, you have to do a little bit of stretching to restore the flexibility of your thinking, and I hope that taking a little time off will enable that. Or perhaps I'll discover that I don't really like being in the office very much and I should do something else with my life. That's a possibility too.

**n+1:** Have you done anything with your days off?

**HFM:** I've actually tried to fix things around the house. So far I've broken—that is, I've tried to fix, but further broken—a toilet and a sink. And I have neutral results on a shower.

**n+1:** Okay, and then there's people not paying.

**HFM:** Yeah, that's more like cleanup. It's probably twice as unpleasant as defense. One of the problems with doing investments that are not in the public markets, doing private investments, is that if one of those investments goes wrong, it can be very time-consuming to manage your way out of it. And in a sense, every time you do a private investment, you're writing a call option on your own time. To make that investment, to monitor that investment on an ongoing basis, takes a little bit of time; if that investment actually goes sour, you're in for a very time-consuming process. And when you're doing private investments, you *can't* make only so many investments that you would have time to try and do recovery on all of them at once. So it's another example of how you have to make assumptions about correlations. People say, "It's never going to happen that all the private investments are going to blow up at once and all these call options on my time are going to be exercised at once." In a sense you're writing more options against your time than you have time, on the assumption that correlation is not 100 percent. It turned out there was very high correlation between all of these private investments. So not only am I doing the unpleasant work of having to do recovery at all, I'm doing it on many more situations at once than I had considered to be likely or even possible.

**n+1:** So you're having a time crisis.

**HFM:** I'm like time insolvent. I declared time bankruptcy. There are situations where you say, "I think I might be able to wring a few more points out of this if I dedicated a lot of time to it, but I don't have the time." It's frustrating. You know there's stuff that you could be doing that would realize value, but you just don't have time to do it, and the stuff you're spending time on is really unpleasant. Dunning people is no fun, dunning companies is no fun, particularly in jurisdictions where you don't have a very strong legal framework. We often structure our deals in ways where we don't have to entirely rely on the legal remedies available in the local jurisdiction to collect, and we are always trying to be creative about the extrajudicial pressure that we can bring to bear. But none of those things is fun to do.

**n+1:** Extrajudicial remedies are . . . ?

**HFM:** For example, things in public relations—you tattle. Some of these businesses rely on confidence. Well, let me make a distinction. There are times when you know that a company simply can't pay. If I recognize that, the company recognizes that, and they engage us in a forthright way, we try to figure out how to recover as much value as possible, recognizing the priority that we as lenders have over the equity holders.* In that case there's no need to bring any kind of pressure. You know they can't pay.

But sometimes there are cases where there's just total chaos in the economy and you have what's called strategic default: The company can pay and they just decide not to because they know that their lenders are busy with other situations, or the courts in their country are so clogged up with foreclosures and controversies that a lender won't be able to bring any pressure to bear for a very long time. That has been, I

---

* A company's capital structure can have several layers. Broadly speaking, the shareholders are the "owners" of the company and are entitled to the company's profits. Companies also raise money by taking on debt, either contracting loans from financial institutions or issuing securities (bonds) in the market. Debt claims are senior to the claims of equity holders; whether the company is profitable or not, it must come up with scheduled payments on its debt or face bankruptcy. If a company goes into liquidation, the proceeds of the liquidation go first to satisfy debts.

would say, rare—rarer than I would have thought in this crisis, maybe just because there are so few solvent companies! Most common is that you have companies that can't pay all that they've promised on the timetable that they've promised or with the interest rate that they've promised, but they *can* pay you a lot. Maybe they can pay you back 100 cents on the dollar eventually but the coupon will have to be a bit lower; maybe they can pay you 100 cents on the dollar, but they need two years to repay you instead of a year. But instead of engaging you in that conversation they say, "Well, I'd rather just pay you nothing. I'd rather just attempt to pay you nothing." And those are situations where you sometimes have to bring extrajudicial pressure to bear.

**n+1:** How do you do it?

**HFM:** Sometimes it's planting articles in the press. We obviously talk to journalists a lot, and they love to hear stories about financially struggling companies. Sometimes it's PR that relates to shareholders: It's embarrassing for controlling shareholders of a company to have it be known that they are not able to pay their debts. It affects the ability of their other companies to borrow because there's like a whiff of doubt. Sometimes it's dealing with their customers or buyers and letting them know that we're going to be able to create legal problems, maybe outside the local jurisdiction, in terms of their ability to import. Maybe shipments will get seized or payments will get seized.

**n+1:** You tell the customers?

**HFM:** I call them up. We know who their customers are, and their customers aren't individuals, they're other companies, so we can talk to them and say, "You better be careful—these guys have stiffed us and apparently there are deeper problems. We're pursuing all the legal remedies we can, and maybe that's going to interfere with your ability to get paid by them."

**n+1:** That's not very nice.

**HFM:** Well, it's not very nice to borrow money from people and not pay when you really can. The main thing is, we're financial professionals, so we should be able to recognize when circumstances bring it about that a company can't pay. And in that case our incentive is to keep the company as a going concern, have a friendly restructuring with the company. And beating them up to no end, there's no purpose to that. But you really have to be careful when you run into a situation where the company sees having a problem as an opportunity to stiff you. If you get a reputation for being a soft or ineffectual creditor it can incent other borrowers you've dealt with to default strategically. Sometimes there's a situation where you have a position that's either quite small or you just assume that you're not going to recover very much, and you just completely go nuts on them in order for other people to see that at times you will go completely nuts and just smash stuff up.

**n+1:** And then you know you won't get a recovery.

**HFM:** Let's say you were going to get 3 cents of recovery: You may as well just smash it up because you'll earn more than 3 cents' worth of fear factor from other borrowers.

**n+1:** What does that look like when you smash stuff up?

**HFM:** You have certain jurisdictions where the bankruptcy process is actually quite destructive of value, so very few creditors will go into the actual bankruptcy process. In that case you might say, "I'm going to take this to bankruptcy. I know I'm going to get zero, but I know you, the shareholder, are going to have a complete mess on your hands. And you're going to get zero and I'm just going to smash everything because I wasn't going to get much recovery anyway." And then everybody says: "Wow, these guys are crazy. They're willing to go into a bankruptcy process in this jurisdiction—nobody does that. That's a suicide mission."

Well, then that's great.

**n+1:** When you say jurisdictions, do you mean in the U.S.?

**HFM:** No, outside the U.S. In the U.S., as much as you hear people complaining about the bankruptcy process in the U.S., that's my wet dream, to go through bankruptcy processes in the U.S. They're so much more fair and speedy and transparent than 99 percent of the jurisdictions I'm used to.

**n+1:** You'd love to go through bankruptcy in the U.S.?

**HFM:** No, I'd love to put people through one. If I could take these defaulting borrowers and put them through a U.S. bankruptcy process, that would make a lot more sense. Even with Obama interfering with the bankruptcy process politically—where the Chrysler secured lenders feel really bad about the fact that they wind up getting 25 cents on the dollar, and some of the unsecured creditors got a better recovery—to me that would probably be a good result. In some of the jurisdictions I deal in, that would be a spectacular result.

**+ + +**

**n+1:** So if you were going to go on offense right now, what would you do?

**HFM:** Well, that's why I'm taking the time off, because it's hard for me to come up with new trade ideas that I really have conviction in. There are a few schematic trades out there that we're doing, but they tend to be in areas where we haven't had—where I haven't had—too many traumatic experiences in the last year. It's very hard for me to find a private lending opportunity right now that I'm excited about, and I don't know if that's because it's just a bad time for private lending. Look, with the global economy doing poorly—even with these odd green shoots—we're still in a bad time. Maybe it's just the case that I'm correct in feeling that one ought not to be doing much private lending right now. On the other hand it could be that I'm just like a dog that's been beaten too much and when somebody raises his hand I flinch. So I find the most opportunities are in areas where I have had good results even in the last year, and that's trading government debt and local interest rates in the markets that I'm involved in—more technical bond-math kind of trades rather than fundamental kinds of trades. And maybe it's just that I'm so tired of dealing with business-people, people in the "real" sector, having spent most of my time dunning them. I'd really rather just deal with mathematical concepts that can't cheat you—at least willfully. If you're deceived, you've deceived yourself.

**n+1:** Were there opportunities in the market late last year that you couldn't take or failed to take?

**HFM:** Yes. In the sense that in December-January there were some very obvious trades in the public markets that aren't there anymore. From the trough we've had a big rally. In the credit markets it's the same thing. There were some very cheap bonds out there and there was an opportunity for people who had risk capital available to buy them, and they've done tremendously well in the past couple months.

**n+1:** And you guys . . . ?

**HFM:** I didn't feel like our fund was in a position where we could ag-gressively take advantage of that because we were playing defense. We were saying, "Well, gosh, what if all our investors want their money back? What if we lose our financing in the repo market? We need to take less risk." That's why the bonds were trading where they were trading. Because many, many people found themselves in the same situation.

**n+1:** And are you mad at your fund for that?

**HFM:** No, I think it was a prudent thing. And it's not like, "God, I was the only one who thought those bonds were cheap and why didn't my partners listen to me?" I'm sure everybody in the market thought those bonds were cheap; they were just buried too deep to take advantage of it. That's why they were cheap. That's why they stayed cheap for a couple months. And as conditions eased on the margin, more people were able to buy, which caused the prices to go back up. It's not like we didn't take any advantage of that. As things started to look a little better we were able to take some advantage, but not nearly as much as if we had known we had loads of capital and we weren't going to face any redemptions at the trough.

**n+1:** So are there no things right now that are at their trough?

**HFM:** The worst valuation discrepancies seem to be past for the moment. They might come back. There might be another shock to the system that causes a massive unwinding of risk. It's a possibility. There's a legitimate debate about whether the equity markets are still attractively priced, whether global credit markets are attractively priced. One area where pricing hasn't really recovered from the shock is the private lending market, and that's why we're kind of ambivalent about lending. It was the case in the past that during the boom, really early-stage companies or small companies or companies with a lot of hair on them would come and say, "I want to borrow, and this is what

I'm willing to pay." And if you said, "No, that's crazy, that's too tight," you'd find out a couple of weeks later that they were able to get the deals done.

**n+1:** A lot of hair?

**HFM:** A lot of hair means a lot of problems. I don't know why we call that hair—hair is good. A lot of warts. Very warty companies were able to borrow. And the mental anchor they had in mind for a fair interest rate had to do with where the public markets were trading, not with the return that they were going to get on that capital that you're lending to them by investing in the business idea that they have. They could have a business idea that would yield 40 percent and it was very risky, but they said, "Well, somebody in the same industry as me issued a public bond at 8 percent, so I'm willing to pay 10 percent but no more than that."

Look, in the past we saw a lot of really dumb deals getting funded, so it wasn't a golden age where every deserving company got capital and no undeserving company did. Maybe it was easier for deserving companies to get capital. But there were a ton of harebrained schemes that used up a lot of capital.

**n+1:** Do you have an example?

**HFM:** Real estate was a great example. Russian real estate. The tallest tower in Europe was going to be built in Russia, and it didn't make any sense: There were no tenants for it, it was a challenge from an engineering standpoint, it was going to take a long time to get done. And they went to borrow money and a bunch of hedge funds snatched it up in no time flat.

**n+1:** Do you know what's happened to that? I actually do.

**HFM:** I think that's gone into default. Certainly the tower's not going forward?

**n+1:** They're making it a parking garage.

**HFM:** Clearly a parking garage is not going to return what a tower did. Or: Every Brazilian meatpacker, every one of the top seven or eight, was able to get enormous loans—these were bonds, not private deals, so maybe it's not a good example. Many of them were just family-run, terrible systems, terrible accounts. They all got bond issues done, and many of them have defaulted.

**n+1:** Why is that?

**HFM:** Many of them were just were not professionally run companies, they were just family-run companies.

**n+1:** They had their meat in the basement.

**HFM:** No, they killed a lot of cows out in the boonies somewhere, but they weren't professionally run, they didn't have good systems, they didn't have controls, the accounts were very squirrelly, a big portion of their assets were tax rebates that the government owed them that they hadn't collected for years. Clearly there was some issue why they couldn't collect them, so that shouldn't count as an asset. But that was the bulk of the assets for some of these meatpacking companies and people still lent them money.

Now there's no lending in the private market. So these sponsors now say, "I'm willing to pay almost anything up to the rate of return on the project in order to get the money to do the project." So the rates are very, very high. On the other hand, the economy is still in a sick state. You have a lot of bankruptcies all over the place; where you have a decent industry but a couple of weak players within the industry go bankrupt, that's going to distort prices in the whole industry. That's an added element of risk of doing this lending business. And if indeed it goes sour and you need to collect, you face the same situation that the mortgage lenders do here in the U.S.: The bankruptcy courts are clogged up with all these other bankruptcies, and the law firm that you may want to hire to handle the legal side of the recovery, they might be booked up.

**n+1:** What kind of companies are we talking about?

**HFM:** You name the industry. It could be a manufacturing company, it could be a small bank, could be something in the agriculture sector, could be a mine. Real-economy companies.

**n+1:** They're manufacturing . . .

**HFM:** Say it's a mining company, and they have a mineral deposit and they say, "This is a very good deposit but I need to develop it." Or maybe there's a mine and it's operating, but it costs them a lot to get the product to market because there's no railway to the mine, so they need to build a railway for it. So that's tens of millions of dollars to build a small railway and now things are much more efficient. "If this investment for us could generate a 30-something percent return in capital, we're willing to pay you a 20 percent return on it." On the other hand, if the commodities prices are very much in flux, buying insurance against fluctuations in commodities prices is prohibitively expensive now because everybody knows commodities prices are fluctuating. It becomes a riskier proposition.

**n+1:** So they were asking for $20 million, say. And it was all from you, or from various people?

**HFM:** From anybody they could find.

**n+1:** And they were offering 20 percent return, meaning you lent them . . .

**HFM:** We would get $4 million in interest per year.

**n+1:** Four million in a year?

**HFM:** Yeah, 20 percent a year, which is pretty high for a project that is not that complicated, and the company wasn't a troubled company in any way. A year and a half ago they might have offered you 8 or 9 percent.

**n+1:** And how long does it take them to pay it back?

**HFM:** Different loans have different tenors. One of the problems with this kind of lending when you're doing it is that it's not an easily tradable instrument and sometimes the tenor is very long. It could be five years, it could be ten years, and it's very hard to feel confident as a lender of your own situation at that time horizon. If your capital is stable enough, then you can commit to an illiquid investment for five years. So that's another big problem with it. And if everybody else finds themselves in the same situation, that's why these guys have to offer 20 percent, because no one wants to get locked into an illiquid loan for three years or four years or five years.

**n+1:** And you made a distinction between the public and the private . . .

**HFM:** With public debt, usually the lenders are bigger, the issues are bigger. You're not dealing with $20 million anymore, you're talking about hundreds of millions of dollars, and it trades. For example, there are dealers who quote a price on the bond every day, there are trades that happen maybe not every day, but a few times per week. So you have some discovery into the price; there are other people looking at the situation, so it's easier to get information. Most important, you can trade it. If I decide I don't want to be in this anymore, I can sell it. Or if my fund finds itself in a situation where we need to raise more cash to pay back investors, I can sell it. With a loan it's a lot harder. It's not a situation other people are following—maybe there's nobody else who's following it—so if you want to sell it, you're going to need to find people, educate them, and convince them that it's actually a good deal. And that's a lot of time and may involve a very high transaction cost.

**n+1:** And the reason they can't go public is because it's too small?

**HFM:** Typically it's too small. Sometimes maybe because there are legal complications that make it difficult for them to go to the public market. Sometimes it's because there's an information barrier: There's disclosure they don't want to make to the whole world, or they'd rather just deal with one lender because they're hairy or there's sensitive competitive information that they feel they'd be harmed by revealing.

**n+1:** So how much of what you do in general is taken up by these?

**HFM:** Our business varied over time, but usually it's been, in terms of capital, between 10 percent and 20 percent of what we do. In terms of time, if even *one* of these goes sour it takes a lot of time to deal with. So it's taking up a lot of my time. In terms of new investment, it's 0 percent now. We're just not doing it.

**+ + +**

**n+1:** What do you think of the stress tests now that they've actually happened?

**HFM:** I didn't think they were particularly stressful. I think the scenarios weren't stressful enough. It's funny how people reacted to it. It was almost like there was this Kabuki theater going on where the market was signaling to the authorities what the market would consider credible outcomes for the stress test, instead of it being an honest exercise. It was like, "Well, it's really important to the market that the stress tests results are good for confidence, and it won't be good for confidence if every bank fails. But it also won't be good for confidence if every bank passes because I know that everybody else knows that not all these banks are healthy. So really the ideal result would be if maybe half of them fail, but not by a lot, except for the ones that it's obvious have a really big problem, and they should fail by a lot so that the stress test is credible. And about half should pass."

So the outcome we got is just the perfect outcome to inspire confidence: not so grim that it hurts confidence, not so optimistic that it destroys the credibility of the stress test.

**n+1:** So Citibank, for example. It failed?

**HFM:** They need to raise capital.

**n+1:** Is that failing?

**HFM:** Yeah. When people talk about a bank's passing, it means it is sufficiently well capitalized to survive the adverse scenario in the stress test. Now, the adverse scenario wasn't necessarily that adverse. Where the economy is today is for some people uncomfortably close to what the adverse scenario is in the stress test. Citibank, under that adverse scenario, would not be sufficiently well capitalized.

**n+1:** How much do they need to raise?

**HFM:** Their requirement was small. Bank of America had the biggest, with $34 billion. Of the nineteen banks, I think nine needed to raise new capital and ten didn't.

**n+1:** Is it going to be hard for them?

**HFM:** If they can't, the government is going to be there to help them raise capital. What happened right after the stress test was interesting: Several of them were able to raise capital immediately. Wells Fargo did an equity offer and SunTrust did an equity offer and they were able to raise capital. That would be an indication that the stress test was useful. The stress tests provided enough certainty about how big the capital hole was that these banks that did have a capital hole could go out and say, "Okay, this is what I need, now I want to raise it, or I want to raise a substantial portion of it." And investors felt confident enough that there wasn't going to be a negative surprise down the road that they were willing to buy into those offerings. Now the question is, did investors believe that there really was certainty about the capital hole? Or is it that investors feel confident about what the government is going to require in terms of capital raising? I think it's more the latter than the former. I think everybody knows there's actually substantial uncertainty about how the economy's going to go—that it might be worse than people expect, it might be better, the banks might need a lot more capital, they might really not need any. But people felt the near-term risk wasn't in an actual capital need, because a bank that has a big deposit base, as we were talking about before, as long as people don't lose confidence in it, it can be insolvent for a long period of time and just sort of earn its way out of insolvency. But what can cause a near-term need to raise capital to turn into diluting of investors is if the government says, or the regulator says, "You're undercapitalized." Now that the stress test has happened, people say, "Okay, I know the government's not going to change its story in the short term. So if I know SunTrust needs $2 billion, that's all they're going to need regulatorily for a while. And to the extent that losses maybe turn out worse than that, they're going to have a chance to earn their way out of it. I'm not going to realize the loss. I'll be able to make myself whole by being a shareholder in the bank as it earns its way out of the pocket."

**n+1:** We thought Citibank was in big trouble, then it turned out Bank of America was in worse trouble than Citibank.

**HFM:** According to the stress test.

**n+1:** So is Bank of America going to be able to raise $34 billion?

**HFM:** I think it's going to be a stretch, but they've gotten off to a good start. They have some assets they could sell to raise capital. They've sold their stake in a Chinese bank. I think there's a chance that they get there.

**n+1:** Are you disappointed that they weren't wiped out?

**HFM:** I have mixed feelings. On the one hand, shutting or intervening or nationalizing any of these banks would have a negative effect on confidence. On the other hand, if it did run itself into the ditch, if in fact it's insolvent, it's a distortion, in a sense, to keep those banks alive, and if they're not well managed, you risk that they'll run up bigger losses in the future and cause more problems. The ideal would be that they be kept alive but radically shrunk. And who knows? Maybe that's the path that the regulators are going to take.

**n+1:** Are they not well managed?

**HFM:** I'm not inside those institutions, so my visibility is limited. When I look at Citibank and my experience dealing with Citibank, it feels to me like it grew way too fast and was way too diversified. Different arms of the institution didn't know what other arms of the institution were doing. That organizational structure was always very puzzling to me, and it felt a little chaotic and out of control. So I think it was poorly managed. You've seen a significant amount of management turnover there. Bank of America? Bank of America itself is not an institution that I did a ton of business with. Where I think that they were poorly managed was with the acquisitions that they made during the crisis: buying Countrywide, which by all accounts was a disaster. They were the poster boys for subprime lending, for supporting politicians with favors, for questionable lending tactics. And Bank of America bought them.

**n+1:** Why?

**HFM:** Who the hell knows? And then buying Merrill in the depth of the crisis. For a lot of money! Not buying Merrill for a dollar. Not taking over the carcass of Merrill once it's blown up. Not buying pieces of Merrill after bankruptcy, like Barclays did with Lehman. But paying a lot of money for Merrill. That's what's landed Bank of America in trouble.

**n+1:** They must have had some idea that there was a lot of value . . .

**HFM:** Yes. But apparently there wasn't. It's like *Let's Make a Deal.* Sometimes you ask for what's behind door number three, and sometimes it's a goat.

+ + +

**n+1:** So what do you see in the next few months?

**HFM:** We're in the middle of a big turn of risk tolerance in the financial markets. The equity markets have rallied a lot, credit spreads have come in a lot, and it's funny how a lot of the economists' forecasts are generated by what the financial markets are doing, rather than the reverse. So now that the financial markets are doing well you hear a lot of talk about green shoots and recovery, and that we're bottoming out. Like after a winter there are green shoots. A botanical metaphor. I guess they've never seen or read *Being There*. There's something a little bit trite about these gardening metaphors. And there obviously is some feedback between the real economy and these financial variables, but it feels to me like in this case it really is these people who work in finance, the equity markets are recovering, the banks aren't failing, and so they say, "Oh, the economy seems to be doing okay." I think it's true that the financial crisis has come to an end for now. We talked about the heart attack. The heart attack ended in the fall, and the latest evidence in the short-term money markets suggests the heart attack is over.* And that certainly has a positive impact.

But the real economy crisis isn't over by a long shot. There still are large misallocations of resources that need to be worked out of the system. For example, there is still a huge number of mortgages that are problematic that need to get worked out. There still are big question marks about whether consumer demand in the U.S. is going to pick up again. These are real-economy questions that haven't been answered yet. And it's very hard for me to believe that with the financial sector in a weakened condition we can have a robust recovery. We are going to see a major change in the savings behavior of the American people. That's a huge change for the global economy. We were consumers of last resort, spending more than we produced. Now suddenly the savings rate has gone positive again. That's a good thing in the long term, but these dynamics are always an issue. Adjusting to that new equilibrium is painful. I don't think that the adjustment to that new, real equilibrium is going to be instantaneous. I think that

---

* The spread between LIBOR and the overnight indexed swap rate, or OIS (an index that reflects the Fed funds rate), is an excellent indicator of the degree of stress in the short-term credit market. The LIBOR-OIS spread, which was under 10 basis point pre–Bear Stearns, stood at 57 basis points on the date of this interview. At the nadir of the Lehman crisis, it shot up to 481 basis points. As of September 2009 it hovered just over 10 basis points.

what you may see is this talk of recovery starts to sound a little bit stale. The recovery is a little bit weak.

And I think this talk will peter out and people are going to realize that the real-economy challenges that we have to look forward to are pretty substantial. The other thing that I grapple with is that there are a lot of reasons to believe we're in a deflationary environment, that we're in a debt-deflation cycle, we've had a negative shock to the price level. The authorities in the U.S. and elsewhere are taking very drastic measures to avoid that outcome: monetary easing, basically printing money, plus fiscal easing. That's inflationary. The idea that they're somehow going to thread the needle and avoid deflation by taking these inflationary measures, but they're not going to go so far as to cause an inflationary spike in the longer run, seems implausible to me. It seems to me we're either going to have deflation, and that's going to be a challenge to our economic performance, or we're going to overdo it and after a period of deflation we're going to have inflation. We've talked about the inflationary U, that after a period of deflation the authorities will overshoot and there will be inflation. And in order to deal with that the Fed will have to tighten, and that means that whatever recovery we have is going to be restrained and we may wind up with another recession down the line before things are finally restored to equilibrium.

**n+1:** Initially you were pretty optimistic about the administration.

**HFM:** They could be doing a lot worse. The fact that there's fiscal loosening going on, they needed to do that. Some of the financial sector policy has been good, some has been bad. It could have been screwed up a lot worse. The outcome has been okay. I tend to be a pessimist when it comes to government. The problem is that Obama's fiscal stimulus is not temporary. Many of the things he's proposing are not likely to be temporary. Like the aid to the states. It's not clear to me that that will ultimately go away. Like the SCHIP [children's

health insurance] expansion or the health care reforms that he's proposing. These things aren't really stimulus; they're more permanent
changes, permanent new entitlements. That's what's a little bit scary.
Some of the things that he's doing on tax policy seem like they could
deter investments. He's taking some steps against supposed loopholes
in corporate taxation that could be very damaging. Now, it's true that
the things he's taking aim against are in a sense loopholes, but they're
loopholes that are there because the overall structure of corporate taxation in the U.S. is very different than in the rest of the world. So to
deal with the fact that we have an eccentric corporate taxation system,
we've allowed these loopholes to be created so that U.S. companies
are not uncompetitive relative to companies from other countries. So
he wants to get rid of these loopholes—that's fine if we're also going
to redo the corporate taxation system so that it's simpler and more efficient and more in line with what's going on in the rest of the world.
But I haven't seen any evidence that that's going to happen. So if you
suddenly make it a lot less attractive to be headquartered in the U.S.,
or, if you're a start-up company, to be domiciled in the U.S., then
that's problematic.

+ + +

**n+1:** So you're taking a mini-break. Have you been looking back at
your career as an HFM?

**HFM:** Of course.

**n+1:** What are your thoughts?

**HFM:** I fantasize about a time machine all the time that would allow
me to go back and not do many investments that I did, and do other
investments that I did in much larger size. So I think back on it all

the time. From a practical perspective, one thing that we've done in my group—and I wanted this done in every group at the fund, but people didn't seem to have much appetite for it, maybe because it's too emotionally scarring, maybe because they think it's maybe not the highest and best use of their time—is to say, "Let's look at every bad investment and treat it like a plane crash." When there's a plane crash they look at the black box, they look at the wreckage of the plane. They have a bunch of investigators come in and they review every step of the flight, starting with the maintenance on the plane before the flight, what the pilots were doing before the flight, what they were doing in the flight. They analyze every step. And they try to see where either policy and procedures were deviated from, or where some of those policies and procedures were wrong, or where the plane design was wrong, and they go back and try to find that problem and change it. And we tried to do this for every bad investment that we did. Not every investment turned out to be a loss, because sometimes you do an investment where the risk/reward is good but you draw a bad card and you lose. But there are investments where we know this was a bad investment, there was not a good risk/reward, and the outcome typically was bad. Sometimes the outcome was good but we were just lucky—*ex ante* it was a bad trade. For all of these you want to go back and do this sort of crash report.

**n+1:** How long have you been doing this?

**HFM:** I think we started about six months ago, and we just finished.

**n+1:** But the trades were over how long?

**HFM:** The past two years. It was a very painful process because we were confronting our mistakes. But we tried to say, "Here were the mistakes, and here's where we need to change our procedures in order to avoid them in the future."

**n+1:** So were you confronting the mistakes of particular people?

**HFM:** I'm the portfolio manager, so they were ultimately all, from one perspective or another, my mistake. Although it could be like I was the pilot, and the guy who maintains the engine was drunk or something. So I wasn't necessarily the primary cause of the whole thing, but I certainly was involved. And ultimately I have responsibility because I'm the pilot or I own the airline or something.

**n+1:** How many people in the group?

**HFM:** About a dozen. We found there were a lot of things that we needed to change. We felt that there were some businesses that we were in that we really weren't staffed for properly. It's like we were flying routes that have to go across an ocean with an airplane that has only one engine. It's not a safe thing to do. So there are some businesses that we decided we aren't going to be in anymore.

**n+1:** Because you just don't have enough . . . ?

**HFM:** We're not staffed appropriately. Maybe it needs more people on the ground than we have, or it needs a different type of experience than we have, or it doesn't fit the capital structure at our fund, or it requires a much longer-term horizon than we have, or requires a more activist investing role than we're willing to take, or more of an appetite for conflict than we have. And there are some aspects of due diligence that we felt like we need to put more emphasis on, and maybe divert some energy from other aspects that we put more time into and really didn't make a difference. There are some jurisdictions where we felt we ought to have a much higher bar for getting involved. We've thought about that a lot.

Then there's the frivolous thinking back, where I say, "I can't believe I did that trade, I wish I hadn't done that trade." Or, "Gosh, I wish I had done that three times the size." There's no good reason to do that, other than that you're a human being and you can't stop yourself. I've been spending too much of my Mondays and Fridays doing that. I have to get past it. It's a big occupational hazard in investing. My first boss told me you can't dwell on bad decisions; you have to learn from them and change the way you do things. It's easier said than done. And the reason he told me that is because he was always dwelling. He knew it was an unhealthy thing.

**n+1:** But you still want to invest.

**HFM:** There are times when I feel like I've been doing this for many, many years, and I have other interests and I'd like to do other things. And I may decide at the end of this working sabbatical that a three-day week was better than five but zero will be better than three.

But I do recognize that there have been times when this has been tremendously enjoyable. There are still times, even now, there are days I have that are tremendously enjoyable. And I do feel that having a good year is very emotionally rewarding. Not just financially rewarding, emotionally rewarding. For all of us, feeling a sense of mastery in a discipline is very emotionally rewarding. And I'm not sure there's anything else I can achieve mastery in. So if this is my only shot I ought to think about getting myself in a good frame of mind, learning from the mistakes I've made in order to be a better investor, so I can get back out there and do it. But there definitely have been more days in the office lately when I'm dealing with some dirt-bag foreigner who borrowed money from me, pissed it away, and doesn't want to pay me anything, and I say to myself, "I have enough money, I don't need this headache anymore, I'm going to work on fixing the toilets in my house."

The financial sector continues to recover while the real economy feels terrible.

In June, the Treasury approves the plans of ten banks, including JPMorgan Chase, Goldman Sachs, and State Street, to buy back the TARP's shares, using the proceeds of successful equity offerings the banks made during the first half of the year.

Governor Mark Sanford of South Carolina, a Republican who had tried to refuse federal aid money to his state before his legislature forced him to take it, disappears for a week without a trace. His family and staff begin to worry. A week later he resurfaces, having been, it very quickly emerges, on a trip to visit his mistress in Argentina, where she is a commodities trader.

In an attempt to boost new auto sales, the Obama administration launches the Car Allowance Rebate System (CARS), dubbed "cash for clunkers" by the press, whereby people trade in beat-up old gas guzzlers for $4,000 toward newer, slightly less thirsty vehicles. Seven hundred thousand cars are sold. The car most often traded in is the four-wheel-drive Ford Explorer; the car most bought under the program is the Toyota Corolla.

On June 25, Michael Jackson dies suddenly. Four days later, a federal judge sentences Bernie Madoff to 150 years in prison. HFM decides to take a vacation.

# HFM VIII

# VACATION PLANS

July 2, 2009
Dow: 8,280.74
Liquid Universe Corporate Index Spread over Benchmark: 251
U.S. OTR ten-year: 3.60 percent
Unemployment: 9.5 percent
Foreclosures: 336,173

**n+1:** So you're going on vacation. This is the first in ten years?

**HFM:** It's my first *long* vacation in ten years. I've taken one day here and there, long weekends from time to time. But let's say a minimum of a full week off counts as a real vacation. So the first one I took was in 1998, the summer of 1998. My girlfriend at the time was going to an academic conference in Rome, and so I'm like, "Okay, I'll go with you." And this was kind of the pre-cell-phone/BlackBerry age. It was difficult to stay in contact. And that week was the week, I think—maybe the week before—Russia got its bailout from the IMF.

So all hell was breaking loose in Russia. We had big positions in Russia and my time in Rome was a tour of the phone booths of Rome. Going from one to the other to call in and hear what was happening and to try to react. So that was a somewhat unsuccessful vacation, let's say. I wasn't happy about it, my girlfriend wasn't happy about it, my boss wasn't happy, nobody was happy about that vacation. The Roman tourist board maybe was happy because I spent a lot of money on a hotel that I really didn't get to use much.

**n+1:** 'Cause you were making calls from the hotel?

**HFM:** Well, no, I was out, trying to be a tourist. But really I was just touring the phone booths. So it was kind of a bust. I sort of soured on long vacations, it became too stressful to be away from the office. The market's always moving, things are always happening. You go away, you're trying to relax, and you just produce more stress because you have the same worries but less information. So I said, "You know what? Instead of having vacation interspersed with work, I'm just going to work for a long time and have a longer retirement. And when I'm retired I won't have to worry about any of this stuff."

I think that's probably not a good strategy . . . and now I'm burned out. So last year, when I was definitely well into the acute phase of burnout, my girlfriend—different girlfriend this time—said, "We really should . . . you know, let's go away." She had a vacation owed to her. And I said, "Let's do this. I have a bigger team now, I can probably afford to step away for a little bit." And we went to Europe, and it actually worked out okay. I was not running from phone booth to phone booth, and obviously the technology's improved, BlackBerrys and cell phones, so it's easier to stay in touch and you don't come home to eight million e-mails that haven't been looked at. So that worked out okay, but a week isn't that long. Really, for a vacation to be relaxing there have to be actual responsibilities that you let go of. At the scale of a week, there are some responsibilities you can let go of, you're not in the office, but if you can stretch that to go longer, there's some whole strategies that maybe you're just going to leave to somebody else.

I've been on a three-day-week schedule, and that's been helpful, but getting away for a long stretch of time was something that I also thought would be helpful and that I hadn't done, really, ever, in the time that I've been here. So we agreed on about a month, on July. And July, sometimes, the summer can get slow in the markets.

**n+1:** Are you going to stay off the BlackBerry?

**HFM:** I'm going to take the BlackBerry with me but I have a very intricate set of Microsoft Outlook rules. There's some huge range of things that if they come in, they're deleted. There's a message that goes out to everybody: "I'm away for the month. I cannot assure you that anything you send me this month is gonna get read. Here's who you need to talk to in my absence."

**n+1:** Microsoft Outlook will delete . . .

**HFM:** Yeah, basically, when things come in, just delete 'em.

**n+1:** What if you see a newspaper?

**HFM:** It's okay. I'm going to read the arts section, and read the movie reviews, sports section.

**n+1:** You don't have any positions on that?

**HFM:** I don't run a sports book. I don't trade on the Hollywood stock exchange. I won't feel any stress about that at all.

**+ + +**

**n+1:** We've talked about—and the Marxists also talk about—the fact that financialization, various financial instruments, have been the engine of growth in the U.S. And as a proportion of GDP, you were saying, those were out of alignment, that there was too much . . .

**HFM:** That the level of profits for the financial sector was too high. If you look sectorially, the financial sector was generating an unusually large share of corporate profits and of GDP. And a lot of that was not sustainable. It was a frenzy of trading that didn't lead to an ultimately productive result. So those are paper profits. And what happened is it turns out that those loans that were extended went bad, or bets went bad, and the huge losses that were recognized were the reversal of those financial sector profits, right? So again, then are you supposed to believe that once that's out the financial sector profits go back to that unsustainably high level? No, they don't.

Another way of saying that is that a lot of that GDP is an illusion.

**n+1:** Would you say that we're going to have a lower level of GDP growth?

**HFM:** A lower level of GDP, period. And the growth may be slower as well because easy credit supercharged that growth. These massive hordes of people that couldn't really afford things, who were buying things—well, you don't have those customers anymore. So you have a lower level of GDP.

**n+1:** There was an item in the *Wall Street Journal* today that Goldman is hiring and that their average compensation is $700,000.

**HFM:** Well, the mean is a very misleading number. There are a bunch of people that make $10- and $20- and $50 million, and there are a bunch of people that get paid mortal salaries. The investment banks, if you look at their, let's call them the traditional businesses, their actually low-risk business, just being the brokering function, they're making so much money this year because a lot of the competition is gone. And there's a lot of disorder in the markets, which means that the spread, the bid/offer spread, it's the spread between where I can go to Goldman and try to sell a high-yield bond and where the person who they sell it to buys it, that spread has widened out because the markets are more volatile. But when people say, "Wall Street's having a banner year," the important thing to note is, it's not that areas of business that were the source of all the windfall profits in 2005 and 2006 and 2007 have returned to those days; it's that other businesses where returns had really shrunk under competition and because of market stability have become profitable again.

+ + +

**n+1:** What do you think of the Madoff judgment?

**HFM:** A hundred and fifty years. You know, as an investor, I'll take the under on that. I don't think he's going to serve the full 150. He's not Yoda.

**n+1:** It's a lot.

**HFM:** It's a philosophical question. We've talked about it at the desk. People say, "How can you put a guy in jail for 150 years? That's *way* more than your average murderer gets." That's true. On the other hand, the whole Madoff thing was so corrosive of trust at just the time when trust was in short supply, that the kind of damage that it did is enormous. So you could say that, in that sense, the consequences are worse than a murder. And you could say that most murders are done in the heat of passion or there's some strong motivation to murder. This guy, he had a perfectly good market-making business and he did this for . . . no apparent reason. He didn't *need* to do this, and in that sense it was more perverse. But how we punish different crimes is a very big philosophical question that's beyond the purview of the mere bond market.

**n+1:** So in a way, the financial professional would tend to want to put him away longer.

**HFM:** You know, when it comes to punishment of financial executives, the average finance professional's opinion as to whether punishment is enough or too much depends on the probability that that particular finance professional thinks he could ever be accused of something similar. For most investors, there's no imaginable universe where they could be accused of doing something like what Madoff did. So people say, "Yes! They should have made it three hundred years! Throw the book at this guy."

But when you look at some of the Enron guys, not Jeffrey Skilling but the guys at Merrill who were charged with helping Enron cook its books by helping set up some of these off-balance-sheet structures or do accounting-motivated transactions—a lot of investment bankers went, "Gosh, I've done some deals that were a little bit like that. These deals were approved by Internal Compliance, and, uh, I'm not necessarily looking so deeply into why the company is looking to achieve a particular accounting objective. Maybe I couldn't see myself doing something quite as sketchy as the Merrill guys did [with Enron]—but I could see having a transaction that could wind up in the papers and somebody opportunistically accusing me of doing something as bad." And so you say, "You can't put people in jail for that! That's crazy!"*

---

* Dan Bayly, a thirty-year veteran of Merrill Lynch, held the post of global head of investment banking when Merrill, at Enron's urging, bought from Enron a stake in a set of power-generating barges in Nigeria. On the strength of testimony from disgraced Enron CFO Andrew Fastow relating to oral assurances he gave to Merrill that Enron would buy back the barges from Merrill at a profit—reflected nowhere in the written deal docs—the Justice Department claimed the deal was a "sham transaction" designed to prettify Enron's quarterly financial results. Bayly did not lead the transaction for Merrill Lynch; it was undisputed that neither he nor Merrill derived any unusual benefit from the deal, and a team of Merrill legal and accounting personnel outside Bayly's control signed off on the transaction. Still,

Or situations where you get the criminalization of failure. Then most finance guys really feel like that's punishing too much. And that's where you get into how everybody in finance hates [former New York attorney general, then governor Eliot] Spitzer, because he's gone after things that were like, "You know, I've seen stuff like this. It's not so different from what happened to me." Even if there is some line that divides what you've seen from what Spitzer went after, it's close enough in appearance. You don't even want to think that just doing your job could land you in jail.

+ + +

**n+1:** You know, sometimes you're like, "Well, looking ahead, I see this and that." But how far ahead do you actually look? What's the time horizon that you think in?

**HFM:** Well, this morning my time horizon was tomorrow when I get on a plane. But the trades that we do, for the most part we're talking about a six-month, a one-year time horizon, though some are much shorter and some are longer. Obviously the longer you look ahead, the more uncertainty there is, the more difficult it is to predict, the more events can intervene. You're asking how far does Wall Street look ahead? Different businesses look differently. Many guys who follow stocks, individual stocks, tend to think about the next quarterly numbers. Then there are people who are strategists, broad strategists, who may look ahead and say, "This is my vision for five years or ten years." Like the people who really jump on this idea of the BRIC countries [Brazil, Russia, India, China]. Those guys are saying, "Here're my thirty-year demographic predictions!"

---

in 2005, he was convicted and sentenced to thirty months in jail. In 2006, a federal appeals court overturned his conviction. The government pushed to retry him, and after years of litigation, his second trial was scheduled for February 2010.

**n+1:** These thirty-year guys, they think about demographics, they also think about global warming, probably, and peak oil even, right? And for you that's not really—

**HFM:** That's not so relevant, because we're not making investments over that time horizon. I'm not charged with building an investment bank in some emerging market and therefore have to figure out which emerging market is going to be a great place to build an investment bank, and run an investment bank in the next ten years. It's not that important to me.

**n+1:** Aren't you investing in emerging markets?

**HFM:** I am, but the trades that we're doing, the time horizon tends to be shorter. It's not like I'm going to build a factory that manufactures cars in India because I think everyone in India's going to have a car ten years from now and I have to have a manufacturing platform there. That's not the kind of trade that we do. The kind of trade that we do would be, well, "I see two companies in India in the same industry, and actually we think they're very similar in terms of financial performance and liability structure, but one of them trades at a much higher spread than the other, so I'm going to buy one and sell the other. And people will come to realize this in the next few months or there'll be an event that forces the market to recognize this in the next couple months." Even though the individual companies might be investing in building factories in the next ten years, in general I'm not wagering on the success or failure of that long-term project.

**n+1:** And how do you find out that one of those companies is better than the other?

**HFM:** We do a lot of research.

**n+1:** Specifically? You send somebody and you say . . .

**HFM:** Yeah, we'll go and visit them, we'll pore through their financials, we'll talk to their customers, we'll talk to their suppliers, we'll talk to industry experts. You know, we'll look for information. We'll try to find an information edge wherever we can.

**n+1:** Okay, how do you choose those two companies?

**HFM:** It really depends. Sometimes we say, "You know what, there's a lot of paper, this is a sector where there's a lot of bonds, we need to learn about that sector because there are probably valuation discrepancies." If you're looking for a four-leaf clover, you look among the three-leaf clovers, you don't look where there's no clover at all, right? So if we want bonds, that's where we're going to do our work to try and figure out if there are valuation discrepancies among those bonds. Or stocks. Same thing. Sometimes it's from visiting countries, you just notice something, right? "There's this financial instrument that I just heard about, it's trading somewhere and it doesn't make sense to me how the high levels are," so we drive out and see if my initial intuition is correct.

**n+1:** Can you give an example?

**HFM:** Uh, let me think back. Let's take one from the late nineties. I went to Bulgaria because we were doing some work on stuff, some trades with Bulgaria, and there was a type of bond called the ZUNK bond. And it was basically like a bond that was issued only locally to creditors of state-owned enterprises that had gone bust; it was a compensation bond. And it was not very well known outside Bulgaria. And it traded at a much higher yield than any of their more well-known financial instruments, so that's kind of strange. Is there some risk that it won't be paid? Is there some tax issue? Is there some reason why a foreigner can't own it? We did all the work and we figured out there was actually a way for us to own it. We found that it seemed like the government intended to pay these bonds and even was looking for ways to retire them early—for example, to let people use them to pay for shares in privatizations. And in the end, they paid, and they were much cheaper than any of the other Bulgarian bonds.

**n+1:** So you got a bunch of . . . ZUNKs?

**HFM:** We got a bunch of ZUNKs.

**n+1:** They were supposed to be paid out to the workers of Bulgaria?

**HFM:** Mostly to state-owned banks, actually, that were the big creditors of the SOEs [state-owned enterprises]. But they made their way to other banks, to brokerages, even to individuals.

**n+1:** So you were just in Bulgaria and you were like . . .

**HFM:** I was in Bulgaria for totally other reasons, and we heard people talk, people in the banks were talking about these bonds, and we're like, "This is kind of strange, they trade on a market." Didn't seem like there was any reason other than information asymmetry that they were trading at what they were trading.

**n+1:** And what advantages did you bring to that trade that, for example, the local banks did not?

**HFM:** They didn't have enough capital to absorb all these bonds. That was the main thing. I think it was clear to them that these bonds would be paid. But when you're a bank, you have a lot less freedom of action than if you're a hedge fund. So each of those banks could only have so much of their capital invested in ZUNK bonds, and their capital isn't big to begin with. Some of the banks that got ZUNKs as compensation needed cash liquidity and they had to sell assets. The Bulgarian banks were quite small at that time. Now they're all foreign-owned, but at the time there just wasn't much of a banking sector there.

**n+1:** And so you went in there and you paid the banks a bit more—

**HFM:** Than they paid for them, or they just needed liquidity and they sold to us. And there are some other foreign banks that got involved in that trade over time, and then eventually there wasn't much of a spread between ZUNKs and other Bulgarian bonds anymore.

**n+1:** Okay. This also happens with a company? You'll go to someplace and there'll be some sort of company that's interesting?

**HFM:** Maybe you go to a country looking at a particular industry and you hear another company mentioned a lot, and think, "I should look at that, I should look at that company." Or maybe you hear a lot of excitement surrounding a certain sector, so you say, "Okay, what's really going on with that sector, and are there interesting trades to do?" We try to be neutral with the sector; we're not just going to take an outright view on a sector, usually. But if there's a lot of excite-ment around a sector, that means that maybe people are just pour-ing money indiscriminately into it, there's some good companies in there, some bad companies, and because we're not focused so much on just riding a sectoral performance trend, we're really concerned about finding relative value opportunities—when people are blindly pouring into a sector, they're not looking so much at the individual details—that's an opportunity for us to go look at all these compa-nies and say, "Actually, you know what? Yeah, people really want to be involved in the real estate sector in Brazil—money's flowing into anything that has to do with real estate in Brazil, but this one company is really great, and this one's a piece of junk, so we want to buy this good one instead of the one that's a piece of junk." The reason that that valuation discrepancy's there is just that there's a flood of money into that sector. And people say, "I'm not going to do the work; I believe so much in that sector's story, I'm going to buy some good apples and some bad apples, and there's going to be a big rally, and I'll have enough apples in the basket that I'll make money on this." We say, "No, we'll go through your basket, and if you're charging the same for all those apples, we'll look and we'll see if there's a worm in this one or that one."

**n+1:** And it's worth it? All that research is worth it to you?

**HFM:** It's a labor-intensive business. In some ways, it's a more labor-intensive business than being able to see a much longer-term thematic investment story, like "I like Brazilian real estate." If I could, maybe if I had an unerring eye for that, maybe I'd prefer to do that business, because it's a lot less tedious detail work and it can be very financially rewarding if you catch those waves. But, to me, it feels like the business that I do is more sustainable because, really, a lot of people don't want to put the time in to do it because the work is tedious. And any kind of a business where you're exchanging tedious labor for money—tedious and difficult labor for money—that business will always be there.

**n+1:** When you say that you're picking one company against another company, that's a directional trade?

**HFM:** That's a relative value trade.

**n+1:** That's a relative value trade. It's hedged?

**HFM:** It's hedged in the sense that it's not exposed to the overall level of the market. Let's say we're talking about one Brazilian real estate company versus another. If tomorrow Brazil snapped off the South American continent and went with the waves, you'd be fine. "I was long in one and short in one—they're both under the Atlantic Ocean now. It's fine."

**n+1:** You didn't actually buy the stocks?

**HFM:** We bought one stock, and we shorted the other stock. So we make money if Brazilian real estate stock A goes up, we lose money if Brazilian real estate stock B goes up. So if the whole sector goes up, well, we don't really care. If the whole sector goes down, well, we don't really care. All we care about is the performance of A relative to B.

**n+1:** So in fact that makes it super-important to distinguish between the two.

**HFM:** That's the whole trade. The whole trade is that distinction. Now, sometimes we do trades where the hedges aren't quite so precise, but we're always striving to only bet on very specific risks. We're not saying, "I think the stock market's going up"; that's not what we do. There are people that do that, and somehow they've developed the ability to sense when the market's going up, or they have some kind of intellectual framework to predict those kinds of movements that are very broad. I don't feel like we have an edge in that.

+ + +

**n+1:** I was reading this book about Long-Term Capital Management.*

---

* Roger Lowenstein, in *When Genius Failed: The Rise and Fall of Long-Term Capital Management* (Random House, 2000), describes the trajectory in the early 1990s of a very high-

**HFM:** Ah, I know Long-Term Capital Management. I got many lectures from my boss in the mid-nineties about "Why can't we be as good as Long-Term Capital Management? We need to be able to generate the same returns Long-Term Capital Management does." Then they blew up and we stopped hearing about Long-Term Capital Management.

**n+1:** There wasn't a lot of skepticism toward them?

**HFM:** There wasn't enough, apparently, given how it turned out. But people didn't have a very long experience with hedge funds—this is before the explosion of hedge funds—and LTCM was very secretive. So all you really saw about these guys was the returns, and who was involved, and the people who were involved all had a really fantastic business and educational pedigree.

**n+1:** And then it blew up and got bailed out. And after that?

**HFM:** Those guys all went in different directions. Meriwether [John Meriwether, the founder of LTCM] started a fund called JWM, which did fixed-income arbitrage and had a number of very good years, and then in 2008 had a horrible blowup, again. It's still around, but it lost a *huge* amount of money. It never, by the way, grew to nearly the size of Long-Term Capital Management. And let alone the funds that became leaders after Long-Term.

So Meriwether, I've never met him, but he was an example that I always cited when I would go and have one of my periodic fits on the desk about how there's no penalty for failure in the investing

---

powered and arrogant hedge fund made up of refugees from Salomon Brothers who used mathematical models to make several billion dollars playing the bond market. In 1998 they lost it all when market volatility in the wake of the Russian meltdown, and the surprising correlation of diverse market factors, went beyond what their models had predicted. The fund, which included two Nobel Prize winners in economics, had to be bailed out by a group of private banks cobbled together by the New York Fed.

world. Which is an exaggeration. There's not *no* penalty for failure, but it's a surprisingly small penalty for failure. When he was
at Salomon, a guy working under him got Salomon caught up in a
scandal relating to manipulation of U.S. Treasury auctions, which
nearly blew up Salomon Brothers; then he started Long-Term Capital Management, which blew up; and gets money again at JWM.
And JWM blows up! So how many times do you need to blow up
before your license to be a hedge fund guy gets pulled? And maybe
that's picking on Meriwether unfairly. But the amazing thing about
that is the incentive structure at a hedge fund is so skewed to the
upside that it seems to me like the only way you could restrain
hedge fund portfolio managers from taking too much risk is either
they have to put a lot of their own capital in the fund or there has to
be a really big penalty for spectacular failure—to constrain hedge
fund portfolio managers from taking advantage of the trader's option, the fact that they get a big chunk of the upside but it's not
their money on the downside. The same is true, maybe even more
true, of proprietary traders at banks. You see people who've blown
up in spectacular fashion go on to get another high-profile job. And
the things you hear are, "I want to hire him; he's learned a very
expensive lesson." Or "He's proved he's a risk-taker." I can't tell you
how many times I've heard that! Yeah, he's proved he's an irrational,
crazy risk-taker!

**n+1:** We're talking about guys who are blowing up, guys who seem
to have a tendency to blow things up or to lose a lot of money. Is it
because they're risk-takers? Or is it because they don't quite know how
to make money in any other way?

**HFM:** There are innumerable ways to blow up. It could be—maybe
you could say this about Meriwether—his business was writing fifty-year flood insurance, right? He was putting on arbitrage
trades, or trades based on historical relationships between financial

instruments, and most of the time, if that relationship widens out, it'll narrow back in again. But every so often, there's a huge crisis and those relationships go to unprecedented levels, and by putting on those trades, really what you're doing is you're writing insurance on that fifty-year flood. And if that's your business, then occasionally there will be a fifty-year flood and you're going to blow up. And maybe, let's say fifty-year flood is the wrong example—let's say it's the two-year flood, right? If that's the case, maybe there is an excess risk premium over the cycle associated with writing insurance for two-year floods, but the way that your return profile's going to look, you're going to make money, make money, make money, and then there's the flood and then you lose a lot of what you've made—but not all. If you're able to play that game over and over again, that should be good for your investors and good for you. If you sized the trades appropriately so that you survive to write insurance for the next flood, you're okay.

But what if you have a lot of guys who are doing that trade, effectively writing two-year or writing fifty-year or whatever flood insurance, and they don't understand that that's what they're doing? You have these blowups over and over because they don't really understand the business they're in.

The other way you blow up is you have people who start in a business that they're good at, and with success they grow and they get into other areas that they're not so good at, and that's a way to blow up. It could be that you have guys who are in businesses and they don't get into other businesses so much as their business grows and they have to add more and more people but they're not good managers, and then you have an operational issue that blows you up. That's a way to blow up.

And then you have guys, you have what you alluded to before, guys who are just truly coin-flippers. They persuade somebody they have the secret to flipping a coin. And you know what? Occasionally heads comes up three times in a row, they make a bunch of money for their investors, they take a percentage for themselves, and eventually tails comes up and that's the end of the road. That's the most infuriating one. There are guys who you know are like that, and they're able to pull this coin-flipping grift more than once. You would think after the first time people would realize that's what's going on.

**n+1:** And one of the things we're seeing now is all these banks that are blowing up or shutting down, they're getting taken over, they're getting nationalized, people getting fired . . . the top management has to go. What happens to those people?

**HFM:** They golf.

**n+1:** Uh . . .

**HFM:** It depends. Many of them wind up, you know, on the beach, but it depends how high up they are. I don't think Chuck Prince has ended up anywhere, the guy who was the head of Citi before Vikram Pandit. If you're high enough profile, any other job would be a big step down for you and maybe you're just old and you retire. But some of these guys wind up at private equity firms where their name can still open a lot of doors, so they're not really investing, but a private equity firm can use their contacts for fund-raising or for finding deals. Some of them go more to boutique advisory firms, same thing. Usually their name, they still have relationships, they have a Rolodex they can monetize. You don't see too many of these very senior guys at banks go and start a hedge fund, but you do see many guys a few layers down at a senior risk-taking capacity at a bank, if the bank blows up, or even their division blows up, they go out and try to raise money for a new fund of their own.

**n+1:** I guess, you know, they make it sound so horrible that these guys got fired, but they're making—

**HFM:** Which? Gimme an example.

**n+1:** You know . . . who was running Bear?

**HFM:** Yeah, his bank completely blew up. Jimmy Cayne.

**n+1:** Uh-huh.

**HFM:** I don't think he's doing anything. He's playing bridge.

**n+1:** But this guy was making . . . how much money was he making every year?

**HFM:** But it was mostly in Bear stock. Those guys were true believers. Say what you will about them, they ate their own cooking. They owned a lot of Bear stock. Of all the investment banks, that company had the highest insider ownership. So, many of these guys, it's funny. People look at some quoted number for their compensation, and it's some large number, but it wasn't like it was delivered in suitcases of cash, right? It was stock options that are valued at a certain price. It's stock and cash, and they use some of the cash to buy stock. And a lot of them held that stock. Now Citi stock's at $3; Bear was taken out at $10. These guys *lost*. Their options wound up being worthless; the shares, a lot of them, ended up being a fraction of what they were worth when they were granted. They walked away with plenty, don't get me wrong, but it's not the same as if you added up all the quoted numbers you ever saw in the *Wall Street Journal*. They usually walked away with a good deal less than that.

**n+1:** Okay, but still . . .

**HFM:** I don't think anybody's crying for Jimmy Cayne. Or for John Thain at Merrill . . . I don't think anybody's crying for him.

+ + +

**n+1:** One of the things I was struck by in the story about Long-Term Capital Management was it seemed to be describing this kind of math bond stuff . . . right?

**HFM:** They did a lot of the bond arb that was very quantitatively orientated, although the sophistication of what counts as quantitative trading today is much higher than the sophistication of what they were doing, and it tends to be more focused on equities, whereas these guys were more fixed-income guys.

**n+1:** It seemed to describe Meriwether at Salomon getting these kind of math guys in.

**HFM:** He was applying a mathematical rigor to those trades, yes. To those relative-value, arbitrage, or arbitrage-like trades.

**n+1:** And a sort of shift in the sort of people who were doing these things.

**HFM:** Oh yeah, yes.

**n+1:** And now we're on the other end of that . . .

**HFM:** I would say most places have the same sort of quantitative resources. Places that try and do trades like Long-Term Capital definitely have quantitative people and high-power quantitative tools. Those may not be the guys necessarily who are making all the decisions, and the decisions still maybe are being made in an intuitive overlay or by guys who are more business guys than quant guys, but the idea that high-power quantitative tools have to be part of the package is pretty well accepted.

**n+1:** My question is, when I was at school, all the football players went to Wall Street.

**HFM:** Yeah, but football players didn't go do what Long-Term Capital was doing. Probably a lot of those guys went into investment banking, meaning advisory work—mergers and acquisitions, or corporate finance advisory, or the part of investment banking where it's really sales. They're going to work on a sales desk at one of these investment banks. I don't think they were going to be quants or rocket scientists— devising these models for trading, or building the quantitative tools that support decisions that traders or investors make.

**n+1:** So you're saying there have always been football guys and math guys?

**HFM:** Well, look, for as long as I've been involved in the business, you've had a wide range of quants and the non-quants. They're not necessarily all football players; you could have people who are just clever intuitives. Whenever one side gets entirely the upper hand over the other: disaster. You need a mix of both.

**n+1:** And the hedge fund world is more . . . ?

**HFM:** It's both. This fund definitely has both. But I think in distinction to various other funds, the two sides do work together very well. We've had our share of problems, but it's never been because the quants ride herd on the intuitives or vice versa.

**n+1:** And you are . . . ?

**HFM:** I'm not a quant. I work well with quants. I have hired very quantitative people to our team, and we are big believers in using quantitative tools, but I myself am not a quant.

**n+1:** Did you not study math?

**HFM:** It was more liberal arts. But I have some training in computer science, and I have some training in math, and I understand what the quants are doing and I can direct them to do what I want to do, but I'm not going to be the guy sitting there and coding up the model. I'm not going to go necessarily deriving every last formula that goes into the model, but I understand what those models are doing and I may say, "This is the kind of model I want and here's how I think you should do it." I know enough to be able to do that.

**n+1:** So you studied humanities?

**HFM:** I did humanities.

**n+1:** And then how did you end up . . . ?

**HFM:** I took some classes that were not, you know, humanities classes.

**n+1:** Did you know in school that you wanted to go into finance?

**HFM:** Oh no, definitely not. Definitely not. I mean, I told you, I'd gotten into finance almost by accident.

**n+1:** How? You didn't tell me.

**HFM:** I was working in a different industry, something similarly semi-quantitative, there was definitely a quantitative aspect to it, but it wasn't purely quantitative. And I was not living in this city, I was not living in New York, and I was looking to move back to New York, and I was about to take another job in industry, sort of like an analytical role in industry. And I had a friend who was working at this particular fund, actually in a quant role, and he's like, "Don't take that other job. We're expanding our presence in New York." He just said I should meet his boss, his boss was starting to get involved in emerging-markets investing. And he said, "You guys are very alike, you should meet. He wants to hire somebody to help him with that business and learn that business and maybe eventually take over that business from him. So just meet the guy." And I did. And we hit it off. I almost didn't take the job; I almost took the other job. I never thought of myself as a *finance* guy, and my view of finance in college, not unlike yours, was that it's for the guys who sit in the back of the class with their baseball cap on backwards, that's what they go and do. So I didn't know that much about what Wall Street was really like, and then I met this guy who became my boss. He was just so smart. He really was somebody who could legitimately be a quant *and* legitimately do the intuitive part of the job. He could have done either, purely. He was that good at both. And I said, "This is tremendously impressive." And the other people I met, who were not what I imagined, that's what attracted me to it.

✛ ✛ ✛

n+1: Let me give you a list of the banks who at the beginning of this book about Long-Term all gather together for the bailout discussions. "For the first time, the chiefs of Bankers Trust, Bear Stearns, Chase Manhattan, Goldman Sachs, J. P. Morgan, Lehman Brothers, Merrill Lynch, Morgan Stanley Dean Witter, Salomon Smith Barney— gathered under the oil portraits of the Fed's 10th floor boardroom . . ."

HFM: They'd be back in another ten years. [*laughs*] Not all of them: Bankers Trust, they were caught in a scandal that they were peddling derivatives to corporate customers in ways that were maybe misleading or inappropriate. That really tarnished their reputation, and then they got hosed in the Russian crisis in '98, and ultimately they had to be bought by Deutsche Bank.

**n+1:** Bear Stearns?

**HFM:** They're part of JPMorgan [Chase] now. And probably that wasn't their plan.

**n+1:** Chase Manhattan.

**HFM:** They bought J. P. Morgan. Now they're JPMorgan Chase.

**n+1:** And they feel pretty good?

**HFM:** Jamie Dimon is smiling like the cat who ate the canary. They're doing great. Of the big banks, they're probably doing the best—of the big commercial banks.

**n+1:** Goldman Sachs.

**HFM:** Goldman's still Goldman.

**n+1:** Uh, J. P. Morgan?

**HFM:** Right, bought by Chase.

**n+1:** Not what they wanted, though.

**HFM:** Uh, no. Look, any of these guys would have wanted to be a survivor, and I think for J. P. Morgan, that's an incredibly legendary investment bank, for it to wind up bought by kind of an unsexy commercial bank, Chase, I know a lot of people at J. P. Morgan when it happened were dispirited, and many people left. And the management team that survived in many of the business units was the Chase management team. But, you know, we're several management teams down the road from that.

**n+1:** Those guys are gone too?

**HFM:** Yeah. I mean, now Jamie Dimon runs JPMorgan Chase and he was not at either J. P. Morgan or Chase at the time.

**n+1:** And a commercial bank is not sexy because . . . ?

**HFM:** Well, look, with Glass-Steagall gone, the barrier between commercial banks and investment banks has sort of evaporated. But commercial banking was considered a less interesting business. You're not taking these enormous proprietary risks the way investment banks are, you're not coming up with these crazy innovations in financial engineering, you're really just, you know, taking the deposits, making your loans to corporates, making mortgage loans to households, issuing credit cards . . .

**n+1:** Handing out free T-shirts?

**HFM:** Handing out free T-shirts for credit cards . . . yeah. Same thing with Merrill. Merrill, in the Bank of America merger, you had a lot of guys at Merrill, saying, "Oh my gosh, I can't believe we now work for Bank of America."

I don't necessarily endorse that view.

**n+1:** Okay. Lehman Brothers?

**HFM:** There's a smoking crater where Lehman Brothers used to be. Pieces of it now belong to Nomura and Barclays.

**n+1:** Merrill Lynch?

**HFM:** Bought by Bank of America, and if you would believe Ken Lewis, that was a shotgun wedding, with the Fed and the Treasury wielding the shotgun.

**n+1:** Morgan Stanley Dean Witter?

**HFM:** They're still around. They have a bank charter now. They are a regulated bank holding company now. They converted from being an investment bank to a commercial bank last year so they would have access to the same kind of support that was available to other commercial banks.

**n+1:** And are they going to do mortgages and credit cards?

**HFM:** They did do credit cards; it's Discover. Discover was Dean Witter, though they spun it off a couple of years ago. But no, they're doing kind of the same business they've always been doing, but they will seek to raise deposit funding. I think that they calculated it much like Goldman, that it was going be difficult to survive and to thrive without having the same safety net of support that the commercial banks did and without being able to raise deposits.

**n+1:** And so they get . . .

**HFM:** They're regulated like a commercial bank.

**n+1:** They're more highly regulated? Different capital requirements?

**HFM:** Yeah. They have to have more capital and they're more highly regulated, but they can take deposits and those deposits are FDIC guaranteed and they have the ability to borrow from the Fed with all the facilities the Fed offers.

**n+1:** Okay. And the last one is Salomon Smith Barney.

**HFM:** Was bought by Citi not long after the events in that book, so they're part of Citigroup now.*

The main thing to take away from that list is there are a lot of quote-unquote "investment banks" in that list. They don't exist anymore. They're either bought, blown up, or converted to being commercial banks.

**n+1:** And this means . . . ?

**HFM:** It's just a big change in the structure of Wall Street. What the practical implications of that are, I don't know; I'll have to see. But we've always had investment banks who've been a big part of Wall Street. When people think of Wall Street, it's that. There is no more Merrill Lynch, Goldman is not a pure investment bank anymore, Morgan Stanley's not a pure investment bank anymore, Lehman is gone, Bear is now a part of JPMorgan [Chase], Salomon has long been part of Citi. There really aren't any pure investment banks anymore. That business model couldn't survive the credit crisis. Perhaps new investment banks will form, or small boutiques will turn into large investment banks down the road. I don't know. They've been such a durable part of the financial system that it is a bit hard to fathom that, you know, they aren't around anymore.

---

* The Smith Barney brokerage business was combined with Morgan Stanley's wealth management and brokerage unit in January 2009. In September 2009, Citigroup confirmed it planned to sell its share of the joint venture to Morgan Stanley.

Over the summer, the real economy remains sluggish and unemployment flirts with the 10 percent level. Foreclosures show no signs of relenting, setting an all-time record in August, and Fannie Mae posts an $18.8 billion second-quarter loss due to rising housing loan defaults. (Freddie Mac posts a modest gain in the second quarter before reverting to form with a $6.3 billion third-quarter loss.) The second Transformers movie, starring Megan Fox and gigantic plastic robots engaged in intergalactic warfare, is released; it is over two hours long and grosses $400 million. Michael Jackson's death is ruled a homicide, and his doctor—quickly dubbed the "Death Doc"—is questioned by police for his administration of a powerful anesthetic that led to cardiac arrest.

Despite all this, financial market variables continue to improve. The S&P500 rises above 1,000 for the first time in 2009 at the beginning of July. The short-term credit market also continues to recover. From a peak of $334 billion at the end of 2008, the Fed's Commercial Paper Funding Facility shrinks to $67 billion at the end of July.

The New York Post reports that after monster first-half earnings, Goldman's bonus pool is on track to meet or even exceed its record 2007 level.

# HFM IX
## FAREWELL

Dow: 9,580.63
Liquid Universe Corporate Index Spread over Benchmark: 185
U.S. OTR ten-year: 3.45 percent
Unemployment: 9.7 percent
Foreclosures: 360,149

**n+1:** Let's talk about your vacation. How was it?

**HFM:** I got to do something that was a little bit unusual for me, and that was to travel around the United States. I travel a lot for work, but it's mostly outside the U.S. And my conclusion is that we have a beautiful country. I happen to live in a very ugly corner of it, but that doesn't take away from the overall beauty of it.

It was also nice to be away from the office for a while. This was almost a month, and it took a little time to get used to it, to get over the withdrawal, the stress withdrawal. I can't say that I went entirely cold turkey. There was a BlackBerry with me at all times, and I wound up doing a decent amount of work.

But we went all over the place, from D.C. to Jackson Hole; I went to Montana, all over Washington state, up and down the coast of

California. I did hiking, kayaking, a lot of outdoor stuff. It was a much more physical existence than I'm used to. My engagement with the world is usually through a flat-screen monitor.

**n+1:** Did you notice interesting stuff in terms of the economy?

**HFM:** I was very interested to see what was going on in the real estate market, and I spent a lot of time counting For Sale signs and looking at brochures. It's not like New York where everything's a co-op and there's a certain amount of secrecy involved when things are for sale. You could just roll up to a house with a For Sale sign and there'd be a stack of brochures under it. The one place where there wasn't *any* sign of distress was Washington, D.C. It's fat times for bureaucrats and politicians; the economic center of gravity has shifted there.

In California it was ridiculous—there were stretches that were just, you know, For Sale, For Sale, For Sale, For Sale, and we definitely saw some of these ghostly, ghostly subdivisions where you could see it was built very recently and mostly unoccupied.

**n+1:** Were you with your fiancée on this trip?

**HFM:** I was, yes.

**n+1:** And so you were like, "Let's check out some abandoned subdivisions"?

**HFM:** It wasn't like we went in search of them. You get off the highway because you're stopping someplace, or you're going to see something, and you can't help but notice a large abandoned subdivision that's brand-new.

**n+1:** California is a place we had talked about that was having a real budget problem, right?

**HFM:** That was interesting, as someone who's worked in an emerging-markets setting. If you went to an ATM while I was out there, there was a message at the end of your ATM session that said, "We're really sorry, bank X is no longer accepting California registered warrants"—I forget what they call them, "registered IOUs." But basically they're not accepting the IOUs for deposit anymore, and I thought back to my time in Argentina, during the crisis there, when you'd go to the ATM, and they'd say, "Do you want pesos or patacones? Are you depositing pesos or patacones?"—patacones being sort of the registered IOU equivalent of the province of Buenos Aires, and that definitely made California feel like an emerging market. But we're a few weeks down the line and they're not issuing IOUs anymore, and the IOUs should actually all be retired in fairly short order, so I guess even California, which still has serious fiscal problems, has at least stepped back from the brink.

**n+1:** What exactly happened in California?

**HFM:** The broader backdrop obviously is that revenues fell off a cliff. California has a tax system that's heavily weighted toward revenues derived from high earners, and high earners' income tends to be more volatile than lower earners' income. So if you have a tax system that relies heavily on high earners' income, in boom years the high earners' income could go up a lot, and revenues increase tremendously—they increase at a rate well beyond the growth of the economy. The downside is that when the economy shrinks, the high earners' income tends to drop pretty dramatically; a lot of people tend to drop out of those high tax brackets, and revenue drops dramatically. California had been through, like the rest of the country, a boom of a number of years, and it effectively assumed that that growth, the growth of revenue, was permanent, and they adjusted their spending accordingly. Then the economy went into reverse, and revenues dropped tremendously, and an enormous budget deficit was opened.

It got to the point where there was no way for California to close its budget gap, and California needs to run a balanced budget, under its constitution, and so the budget couldn't be passed, and without the budget being passed, California didn't have borrowing authority, and it's not clear even if it did have borrowing authority, whether there were going to be any willing lenders to California in the size it needed in the absence of a budget, and so it just didn't have the cash to pay some of its expenses. And so instead of paying suppliers in cash, it gave suppliers these IOUs, which it would redeem for cash at some later date. In effect, it was forcing its suppliers to become lenders to the state of California.

That's happened in the past to California, so this isn't the first time, but the last time it happened it was clearly going to be for a short time and it was of a small enough size that banks were simply willing to accept those IOUs for deposit as though they were money. They paid a little bit of interest, and that interest was enough to compensate the banks for those IOUs that they had to hold. But in this case it wasn't clear when it was going to end, so banks at a certain point stopped accepting them for deposit. People who were paid those IOUs just had to hold them; you just had to wait in line to get paid. It was really an interesting illustration of public choice theory, to see who got paid the IOUs. Employees of the state, including the state legislators themselves, got paid in cash through this whole experience. It was really the suppliers, outside contractors, who got paid in IOUs.

**n+1:** And were suppliers mad about this?

**HFM:** Oh yeah! And in fact they discovered to their chagrin that even though they were paid in these IOUs and not in cash, they owed tax on that revenue as though they'd been paid cash, and they had to pay in cash, they couldn't pay in California with the IOUs. They wouldn't accept them.

**n+1:** Wow.

**HFM:** So that puts you in a bit of a pickle, right? You've been paid these IOUs and you have a cash expense to pay tax on that, so what are you going to do if you're a small business? You have to go try to borrow in some way, so it imposed a real cost on a segment of the California population. At this point the IOU experiment, at least the issuance of it, is over, but while I was out there they were still being issued and it wasn't clear when the issuance was going to stop and when they would be redeemed.

**n+1:** But now they've been redeemed?

**HFM:** I don't think they've been redeemed yet. I think California is close to taking out a loan that would allow them to redeem them.* But definitely the budget is now passed, so there's less doubt on California as a credit. And obviously the financial markets are in a much more risk-tolerant mood, so finding a willing lender should be quite a bit easier now.

**n+1:** Were there any places that you were really amazed by that you would recommend?

**HFM:** I loved the Olympic Peninsula in Washington, Olympic National Park. It's quite close to Seattle but it's an entirely different kind of landscape: you can climb these really enormous peaks and be able to look down at the Pacific Ocean, or look down toward Seattle, or look all the way east and see the Cascades.

**n+1:** And they're still there, they haven't succumbed to the crisis?

**HFM:** Yeah, no matter what the stock market was doing, those mountains were still there.

---

* California opened the process for the redemption of IOUs on September 4, 2009.

I'll tell you this, though: The hotel business is also hurting. It was interesting to see that really none of the hotels we went to were sold out or particularly crowded, and I was changing our itinerary a lot, in the days running up to actually leaving on the vacation, and it was just easier online to cancel my reservation and make a new one, and every time I'd cancel my reservation and look, you know, the prices kept going down. It was *great*. They were having trouble filling these hotels up.

**n+1:** So you recommend last-minute reservation buying these days.

**HFM:** It worked for me. You look at the markets doing well again, maybe those days are over. But there was at least a brief moment there where we travelers had the run of the hotels.

**n+1:** Somebody was telling me recently that he stayed at a fancy hotel and then they charged him for the gym. Did you notice this happening?

**HFM:** You know, some hotels do that. I would basically make like a 1970s rock star in that room if they tried to charge me for the gym. I'd be smearing feces on the wall, I would buy an electric guitar just so I could smash it through the window. It's outrageous! They're going to charge you for the gym. What's that all about? I'm pissed off. I've definitely seen places that do that. It's an injustice.

**n+1:** [*laughing, trying and failing to talk over heated HFM*]

**HFM:** It's an affront to common decency.

+ + +

**n+1:** Okay, okay. You returned to New York. What did you find?

**HFM:** That the mood had improved substantially even from the time I left. The last time we spoke, the mood in the financial markets had mellowed; now it's almost like, within the financial markets, everything's back to normal. You look at credit spreads, they've retraced a lot of their widening; obviously the equity markets aren't back where they were, but volatility has fallen, and the indices are higher, and all the measures of the functioning of the guts of the credit market are all kind of back to normal, you know, the spread between LIBOR and Fed funds has come back down to levels that we hadn't seen since the Lehman collapse. Even the Fed's balance sheet is stabilized, you're not seeing this massive money creation anymore. So it feels like in the heart of the credit market, the heart attack thing is over, the credit heart is beating again.

Now, what's going on in the real economy is harder to gauge. The financial markets led this crisis, they've come out of the crisis first; the real economy has a lag, but even the real economy at least has stopped falling, and even has bounced back in some sectors, and all of these arrows that were pointing down are now sort of starting to come back to neutral or even pointing up. With the exception of the labor market—and people always talk about the labor market being a lagging indicator, but unemployment is still very high and is continuing to go higher. And I think the markets, their mood is obviously much more affected by financial variables than real variables, so I think you'll find people on Wall Street feeling more cheer than the average guy on the street outside of New York.

**n+1:** As usual!

**HFM:** As usual. Not for the usual reasons that they're lapping up the cream of the continent, but because their sector has stabilized first. But the labor market is still hurting, and getting worse. That is the big question mark for whether this bounce-back is going to be a sustainable resumption of economic growth or whether it's going to be something that stalls out.

**n+1:** What does that mean that it's a lagging indicator?

**HFM:** Demand recovers first, and that starts to soak up excess capacity in the economy, which stimulates business investment, and that starts to stimulate hiring. So hiring is kind of the last thing to happen when you go through a recovery. Companies don't hire unless they believe a recovery is really sustainable; they'll just work people longer hours, they'll try to get more out of their existing employees, and only when they are convinced that recovery is sustainable and sustained, then they go out and hire.

But when you're talking about unemployment being as high as it is today, you now have all these feedback mechanisms, right? Can recovery be sustainable if unemployment is at 10 percent? Because unemployment at 10 percent creates a big drag on the housing market, and that creates a big drag on confidence, and it winds up retarding the recovery itself.

**n+1:** It seems like people being out of work, you know, it's pretty much the worst thing that could happen to them . . . .

**HFM:** And it destroys their ability to consume, and it destroys not only their willingness to consume but other people's willingness to consume. It creates a sense of insecurity even in people who still have their jobs.

**n+1:** And what exactly are we talking about, then? What are all these positive indicators? What are they based on?

**HFM:** Well, human beings evaluate most of the world relative to history or relative to expectations. A lot of the positive indicators have to do with "consumer confidence," but really it's just that people had it in their heads, right, had it beaten into their heads by hysterical people in the press, or by people who happen to have an honestly held, very bearish view, like Nouriel Roubini, that the world is coming to an end. But after a while when you wake up each day, the sun still rises, there's still food, it's not *Mad Max* with Australian guys with mohawks driving up and down the roads killing you for gas . . . and people start to feel better.

The other thing is that it's very hard for the economy to shrink forever without new shocks, so it's sort of self-correcting. Economic activity drops, but in the end people still want to innovate, they still want to make money, and so their economic activity persists and recovers. Unless you're talking about somebody bombing us or something, the economy's not just going to shrink and shrink and shrink without end.

**n+1:** Can we take a concrete example of what's going on where there's economic activity that's generating some of these positive signals that you're talking about, but not jobs? What would that look like?

**HFM:** If you look at the auto companies, they're not hiring, right? But because the guts of the credit system are functioning again, car loans can be issued because car loans can be securitized again, so cars are being sold. Now, you were selling 16 million units a year during the boom, that was clearly unsustainable, but for a while there it was on pace to be running at 8½ or 9. Now that there's actually some credit available, now that there's "cash for clunkers," now you're running at a rate that's 11 or 11½. But these companies aren't going to hire on that basis—they were still behind the curve in firing, probably. But that does count as an uptick in economic activity.

Chrysler just wasn't running, right, because they weren't sure what was going to happen with their bankruptcy. Well, now the factories are running again, but the idea that they needed to be scaled to sell a certain number of vehicles that they were selling at the height of the boom, that's not going to come back for a very long time. All those people who were autoworkers, they need to find employment in some other sector, which is a slow and difficult process—the process of matching labor that was in one sector, which is really never going to need it anymore, to another sector. Construction is another example of that. There was nothing happening because the credit market ground to a halt and there was total panic. Okay, now you might've seen that new home sales rose for the first time in a while recently. So people are dipping their toes back in the water. But we're not going to be selling homes at the pace that we were when there was this absurd mortgage bubble going on, and therefore people who were employed doing construction, they're going to need to be deployed somewhere else. And that's a slow and difficult process, because people are not—much as sometimes capitalists are accused of thinking of people this way—they're not interchangeable widgets, you can't take a construction worker and just apply him to any old other industry. There are skills that need to be acquired, maybe there are issues of location and geography that are barriers to finding a job, and that sectoral reassortment, there's a lot of friction involved in that, and it causes unemployment to be sticky.

That could make the recovery very weak, or could even drag us back into recession, if there's another adverse shock, or if you had more problems with bank failures, or if people lose confidence because of the fiscal situation in the U.S., or any number of things.

n+1: How much of the recovery, insofar as it's begun, has to do with what the government did in the past year?

HFM: Well, you can't run controlled experiments with economies, so that's a hard question to answer with quantitative rigor, but if I consider it from the position of somebody who's trading the markets, for sure the actions with respect to the financial sector have something to do with the speed with which the crisis abated. So all the actions the Fed took to pump liquidity into the market, the TARP, particularly the rescue of AIG and Citi and Bank of America. The fiscal stimulus: it's hard to make a case that the actual spending in the fiscal stimulus has much to do with it, because not that much has been spent of the stimulus package itself. However, government policy doesn't work, or fiscal stimulus doesn't work, only through actual deployment of dollars—it does it through the expectation channel. If people know that government money is coming, if you're a company that does infrastructure building and you know that there's lots of government money coming to infrastructure, you're going to be slower to lay people off, and you're going to be more confident. So that has had some effect.

If you take the more pessimistic view, you can say that all that the government action has done—it doesn't really solve anything, and it doesn't really repair the losses that were caused by the irrationality of the bubble—is really shift the consequences temporally, in the sense that the Fed and the Treasury have done a lot of things that stabilize the situation today at the cost of problems down the road. Maybe they've cured an acute problem today by trading it off against a chronic problem down the road. And the acute problem is financial collapse that could lead to a debt-deflation spiral, and they've cured that acute problem. But the cure is not without its side effects, and the side effects are exacerbating our chronic problems, which are the chronic problem of a weak fiscal position, and potentially the chronic problem of inflation.

**n+1:** I guess one of the things that's a little hard for me to get my head around, and I want to say any layperson, but maybe just me, is that it seems like every business that's run, is run on credit.

**HFM:** Yes.

**n+1:** So nobody actually has, they never have, the money on hand that they're going to need in a certain amount of time?

**HFM:** Well, what does it mean to have an enormous mound of cash sitting around? I mean, is it like in the executive suite, it's like the pool that Scrooge McDuck has, with gold coins, and he swims around in that, and when money is needed he takes gold coins out of the pool and uses them to pay for things? I mean, what is a pile of money? A pile of money is, for example, a deposit at a bank. Okay, well, what is a deposit at a bank? The bank's supposed to lend that out to somebody. So a cash balance is . . . one company's cash balance eventually works its way to be credit, it's credit to somebody else. The point is that, you say a company or a person has cash sitting around, what does that mean? It means that they have consuming power, that they've moved consuming power intertemporally. It means that they've produced more than they've consumed in the past, so they have a right to consume more than they're producing at some point in the future. So that just means that some party has a claim on another party. It can't be that all of us as an economy, that we all have lots of claims on future consumption and none of us have any debt. Otherwise you would have an economy that's entirely demonetized, it would be entirely equity, you know, we would just have claims on capital goods or on ownership of companies. You know, if you want to have money that's not just dead pieces of paper that will be worth nothing if everybody tries to spend it at once—really my money, through an extended chain of financial relationships, is somebody else's debt, it's a credit to somebody else.

**n+1:** Individually—everyone with a mortgage is in debt, right?

**HFM:** Yeah. And their debt is to banks. And the other side of that is asset-backed securities and mortgage-backed securities that individuals may hold or that may be held by banks, and on the other side of that is the bank's liability, which is a deposit which you treat as money. The credit system breaking down is the line between what's considered money and not money moving, so that people, the only thing they want is that pool of gold coins that Scrooge McDuck swims in, and there just isn't enough of it to go around. And therefore a high-quality company's promise to pay in sixty days—commercial paper—which was the other side of something that I consider money, suddenly that's not acceptable to me, I just want treasury bills, or I just want gold. There's just not enough of that around for people to be able turn the things that they used to consider money into the things that they now consider money.

**n+1:** And so when things are going well, there's just a certain number of entities—I guess mostly corporate entities rather than individuals, although all the individuals have debt in the form of mortgages—where people owe more money than they have, and yet it's okay somehow.

**HFM:** It's okay because they have an asset. Their earning power is an asset, right? I'd be willing to lend you money, and you spend it to buy something—you know, maybe you spend it to go to Vegas and gamble—but I know that you have earning potential, and so you'll be able to pay me back. So it's turning something that's totally notional, right, that doesn't have an immediate ability to be turned into cash, but it has value, right? The fact that Keith Gessen says "I promise to pay you back in a year from my Vegas gambling bender" has value. And I consider that claim—maybe it's mediated through a bank or a credit card company; you know, the credit card company loans you the money to go on that bender—and I buy a note of that credit card company, or the credit card company's bank, and I have a deposit at that bank. But really, what do I have? I have a claim on Keith Gessen to pay me in a year, when he gets better at poker. Or gets a book advance or whatever.

**n+1:** Uh-huh.

**HFM:** And in good times, I'm perfectly willing either to just allow that illusion to work on me, or if it's not illusion, if I know what's going on, to consider that to be money, right? It's sufficiently atomized and diversified—there's a million Keith Gessens, you know, making a million promises, and I have some slices of that. But when the economy turns down, well, first of all, maybe you're not going to be able to earn, so what I thought was money isn't money anymore—for real, because you can't pay. Or it's just that I don't trust that you can pay anymore, and I want to exchange that claim that I had on you for something that's more ready money, like dollar bills or pieces of gold or treasury bills.

And if everybody wants to do that, well, there are all these claims on Keith Gessen and only so many treasury bills, so what do you think the exchange rate is between treasury bills and claims on Keith Gessen? And who's going to make a new loan to Keith Gessen if the value of that in terms of real money has sunk to 20 cents on the dollar? You wouldn't go and make a new loan, because you'd be taking something that's valued at a dollar and creating for yourself something that's worth 20 cents. So credit just stops.

**n+1:** And yet at the same time, what happened a few years ago is that people were looking at these loans, and they said, "Oh, these loans are just lying around, or they're underutilized"?

**HFM:** Well no, it wasn't the loans that existed, it's that they created more loans. They said, "Oh well, I have money, okay, I want to earn more with it, what should I do? Oh well, you know, I can buy this asset-backed paper that's rated triple-A and get a nice yield on it." Well what's the other side of that? The other side of it is that somebody says, "I gotta make that. There's a bid for this paper, I need to manufacture it. What do I do? I need to go out and make loans. I originate loans. I turn that very notional asset, that promise, somebody's promise to pay you in a long time, into real assets." So the person promises to pay;

that creates money. That money is used to pay somebody to build a house, so effectively it turns into a house. And all these houses are built for people whose promises to pay simply are not worth what they were given in return. And that's destruction of value. But while it's going on, all these houses are being built, and so these builders and construction workers are doing great, they're depositing money in the banks, the banks have more money than they need to do something with, so they buy up more of that asset-backed paper, and more mortgages get created, and on and on until the point where there's no more people we can give mortgages to, or there's some sort of exogenous shock that causes this expansion to stop, and the machine doesn't work unless it's expanding. In a sense it's a bit of a Ponzi scheme. I mean, a lot of economics has the dynamic of a Ponzi scheme—it really only works when you're expanding.

Once it goes into reverse, then you get the experience that we had in 2008.

+ + +

**n+1:** Now that things have improved . . . now that we're recollecting in tranquillity, what is some stuff that strikes you as scary and crazy from a year ago?

**HFM:** I think I've told you. I don't think there was anything that I was blocking out at the time. It is funny, though. I'll tell you this: It's funny how quickly people forget. One of the things that was very noticeable before the crisis was that banks had been very willing to do derivatives trades with a hedge fund like ourselves with very little margin posted by the hedge fund. So, for example, generally it's like Goldman and AIG, right? A bank would come to us and say, you know, "Hey, we're long exposure to company X. Do you want to get long exposure to company X, take that exposure from us?" In other words, "Do you want to write credit protection on company X?" And if we said, "Yeah, sure, we want to do that"—let's say we're writing credit protection on company X for ten years, and it's a fairly risky company—the bank would take an initial margin from us, so we would have to post some money to ensure that we would make good if the company defaults, and so that if tomorrow we go belly-up, the bank would have enough cash so that if they have to go replace that hedge in the market, they would have money to cover their losses.

**n+1:** Wait, aren't they trying to trick you? Why would they say, "We bought this thing and maybe you want it"?

**HFM:** Maybe they originated the loan, and the company needed a $300 million loan, and they only have the risk tolerance to keep $100 million themselves. So they need to hedge $200 million. So they're going to stay exposed themselves but they need to share the risk around.

In the crisis suddenly it became a salient question: "All these banks, their risk has been reduced by buying credit protection from counterparties like hedge funds or AIG, and they've only taken very small amounts of margin, so that if those hedge funds or AIG goes belly-up, these banks, there's no way they'll be able to go out and buy protection without losing much more than the margin that they've taken from their counterparties, and these banks will wind up sustaining enormous losses." So the banks just radically changed their policy on how much margin they would take. Deals where if we wrote a million dollars in protection they used to take $30,000 or $40,000 in margin, they were now asking for $200,000 or $250,000 in margin—in other words, 25 percent of the exposure.

And everybody said at the time, you know, "Gosh, this whole idea of hedging through derivatives, it's really flawed if counterparties are really only taking a very small margin from each other." And now we're only six or seven months from the nadir of the crisis, and we're working on some trades recently, and we're like, "What's the margin on that?" And it was back to $20,000 or $30,000 of margin.

And I always used to think that the reason that financial markets' memory is so short is not because individuals are shortsighted or they easily forget lessons bought at very high cost, but that the average life of an investor is kind of like the life of a mayfly. I mean, they just turn over really fast.

**n+1:** They die?

**HFM:** Not their life as a person, their life as a trader. They become a wonderful butterfly and a philanthropist, and then some other caterpillar trader takes their place.

But in this case, it's not different people, *it's the same people*. And honestly, for me it's quite hard to understand how those lessons have been forgotten so quickly. And it makes one wonder whether those people who blame lax practices like posting very low margins on derivatives, those who characterize that as a product of markets and banks being greedy, of guys just wanting to do a loan and lay it off and they don't really care that they're laying it off on a counterparty that won't ultimately be able to make good, and they don't care 'cause they won't be there or they'll get paid a bonus before it happens . . . I tend to be a little skeptical of that view, but gosh, the fact that people are doing the same thing certainly gives some weight to that view.

**n+1:** And so do you say, "No, why don't we give you some more money"?

**HFM:** [*pause*] No, I wouldn't volunteer that. But internally we reserve more capital against that position. I don't want to give money to some bank, because I don't love the bank's credit necessarily, right? So why should they be holding on to my money? I feel like, I'm as good a credit as the bank. However, I do believe that the position is riskier than what the margin requirement reflects.

If I only have to give $20,000 to the bank for that position, I'm going to keep $80,000 or $100,000 of liquidity available because I think the position has risk, it could move that much against me, easily, and I have to have that money available. Now, if the bank were more prudent, the bank would want to make sure of that, and the way that it would make sure of that would be to hold on to the money itself. But I'm much happier, I'm much gladder to be able to keep it, to hold on to it myself, rather than give it to a bank that may not be a perfect credit.

**n+1:** Do you keep it in a bathtub in gold coins?

**HFM:** I keep it in a gold swimming pool under my house. And I swim in it and cackle and talk like Scrooge McDuck.

**n+1:** But presumably there are other institutions that are not as prudent as you and that are once again not doing this.

**HFM:** Yeah, I think there are many institutions that treat the margin requirement that the bank charges as a good indicator of the risk of the position they're taking on.

**n+1:** So these guys, when they set a low margin requirement, it helps them just put the deal through, and then they get paid.

**HFM:** Yeah, because even if I believe that I should have $100,000 of liquid capital available against a position, I would much rather post none of it to the bank if I can avoid it. So it's much easier for the bank to get the business done, it's easier for the trader at the bank or the salesperson at the bank to get it done, if he can persuade the credit department of the bank to ask for less margin.

And on the other side of it, if I'm a hedge fund guy who's reckless and just trying to make as wild a bet as possible, because my compensation arrangement might encourage that, well then, gosh, I would love to post as little margin as possible, so that I can have this big position—the less margin I have to post, the bigger the positions I can theoretically run on a given amount of capital, so the universe of willing counterparties for a bank expands the less draconian its credit policies.

**n+1:** So you're saying that these crazy, highly leveraged bank salesmen have emerged from the rubble again to perpetrate their—

**HFM:** Not at every bank, not at every bank. Some banks have moved much less from their policies in the depth of the crisis than others. But it's surprising that a number have gone back to policies that look very much like the policies that they had before the crisis.

**n+1:** Well, shouldn't we call the police? The regulators? Why aren't the regulators looking?

**HFM:** I think the regulators . . . I don't know. Maybe they haven't gotten to these guys yet. Maybe there are bigger problems at these banks that they're busy controlling. But it's just surprising to me.

**n+1:** Me too!

**HFM:** Hey, look, this is one of the things that convinces me that you can't have a system that relies on the regulators being incredibly intelligent to control risk. You need blunter instruments.

**n+1:** In this case that would be . . . ?

**HFM:** In this case maybe it is forcing many of these derivatives to be on exchanges that have very blunt margin policies. Another thing is just making sure that the rules that govern whether a hedge actually reduces a bank's risk need to reflect the possibility that those hedges may not hold up. It's too hard for the regulators to look at the minutiae, like "What's the margin policy for hedge fund X?" That's too fine-grained. So you say, "You know what? We're just going to assume that there's some risk inherent in making a loan to company Y and buying protection on company Y from a counterparty. That's not a zero-risk position."

**n+1:** 'Cause otherwise it's like in *Alien*. They killed all the aliens—

**HFM:** You can't kill all the aliens.

**n+1:** But there's this alien out there that's back to lending!

**HFM:** It is frustrating. The other source of frustration is—I don't wish ill on my fellow finance workers in New York, but it is surprising to me that we're seeing hiring again at some of these banks and not-small compensation packages attached to that hiring. And I'm starting to get calls from headhunters again. It's kind of surprising. You would think that the banks would be a little bit circumspect about leaping back into some of these businesses. But it's funny: Some of the banks that were unscathed, or less scathed, by the crisis—some of these banks that were less prestigious had a hard time hiring these highflyers. Now they're taking advantage of this to bulk up, and to give the same kind of big deals to traders and to investment bankers that their more prestigious cousins were giving before the crisis.

**n+1:** Amazing.

**HFM:** And it's kind of galling. It is a little galling!

+ + +

**n+1:** All the more reason, then, for me to return to my question. We need to remind people what it was like during the scary months, because, okay, you told me a story about your colleague that you ran into who was withdrawing—

**HFM:** Who was withdrawing the money from Citi, yeah.

**n+1:** And you told me that the scariest moment was when they delayed, when they voted down the TARP the first time.

**HFM:** Yeah.

**n+1:** But, you know, what else was scary at the time?

**HFM:** Well, coming in every day, hearing about another fund that was blowing up, or another rumor about a bank blowing up, many of which turned out to be false, but you think about, "What's my exposure to that bank? Oh my gosh, if that happens I'm going to lose this amount of money. And if I lose that amount of money in normal times that wouldn't be lethal, but then maybe the banks, the other banks that I'm relying on for financing, will pull my lines, and . . ." I definitely had many sleepless nights which turned out to be pointless worrying, but you can envision these very extreme scenarios, where yesterday I was sitting at a very conservatively run, stable fund, and tomorrow, because of panic, we're out of business. You'd have to imagine a concatenation of very extreme events for that to happen, but you were seeing some of the first links in that concatenation happening each day, and rumors about the next links possibly happening, and you go from something where it's a 1 percent chance of this, of link one happening, and a 1 percent chance if link one happens that link two happens, and all the way down the chain, so that the probability of a catastrophic result is infinitesimal. Suddenly you see link one go. You're like, "Holy cow. Six months ago I thought that was a 1 percent probability, but now it's just happened. Well, maybe the next link isn't a 1 percent probability, it's a much higher probability, and now if I multiply all these probabilities together, there's like a meaningful probability that we could get blown up!"

So that was pretty scary.

**n+1:** So you would get in in the morning at what time?

**HFM:** I get in, you know, five-thirty, five forty-five.

**n+1:** Whoa. And there were already people in?

**HFM:** There weren't necessarily people here. But I would talk to London, and the people in London say, "Oh, did you hear a rumor this bank is in trouble? Or this fund, they're being liquidated, their prime brokers are liquidating them." I mean, every day there would be some crazy rumor like that. Sometimes they'd be true; mostly they'd be false.

And then you'd get calls. Like, say, one thing that's scary is, what would happen to our financing? Like every hedge fund, we are reliant on financing from banks; we're leveraged. Our leverage is very low relative to other hedge funds. So we're probably about the most safely positioned hedge fund you can imagine. It's meant that our returns have sometimes been lower than our competitors', but we feel like we've minimized the risk of a catastrophic blowup to about the lowest level you can have for a hedge fund. But even so, we do rely on financing, on banks for financing. And we had to come up with all sorts of contractual arrangements, back in the calm times, to make it impossible for that financing to disappear overnight. And that had required a lot of work on our part, and it had a cost, but we felt it was worth it, to be prepared for potentially bad times.

But sometimes during the crisis we saw banks trying to back away

from or even renege on those deals. The fact that they had committed to locking up that financing for a certain amount of time—they
didn't care! It was interesting—we had an arrangement that related
to a very narrow asset class that I trade, I don't want to get into too
much detail, and the amount of financing that was being provided
was actually very small, it was on the order of tens of millions of
dollars. And it was an arrangement where the terms of that financing couldn't be changed except with six months' notice, and they
just called up one day and said, "We're changing our requirements,
we're changing our margin requirements, we're multiplying them
by three or four."

And it was funny—we had so much extra liquidity, because we
were managed very prudently, that we could just meet that. But this
was a commitment that they'd made, a contractual commitment.

"You've made this contractual commitment."

"Well, we don't care, we're changing the rules."

**n+1:** And?

**HFM:** In the end, we paid them the money. In fairly short order we
found another bank, actually more than one bank, that was willing to
give us a better deal, that looked more like the original deal that we
had with the first bank, and we moved the positions over to that bank
and terminated the arrangement with the first bank. But if that happens once, it's something that you consider pretty unimaginable, because it was a contract. And then you say, "Well gosh, let me think of
all the other financing arrangements that we've done, where we think
we've protected ourselves by, you know, getting guaranteed terms for
that financing, so that it can't be canceled on short notice . . . if this
one can be canceled, what if these ten others are canceled? What do
we do then?" Our whole liquidity planning was predicated on the idea
that these banks will actually honor their contracts.

**n+1:** You were continuing to receive financing from them, is that right?

**HFM:** Yeah, yeah. But let's say, you know, for $100 million of positions in this asset class, we had in the past had to post, you know, $5 million. And maybe internally we had reserved $5 million more, because we thought that $5 million was too low. Suddenly they're saying, "You need to post $30 million." And we had plenty of cash, it was fine, we could do that, it wasn't going to sink us, but if every single financing arrangement we had did that, then we would be in a very distressed position.

**n+1:** Is that legal? Can they do that?

**HFM:** They couldn't, but it's like, what are you going to do?

**n+1:** Can't you sue them?

**HFM:** They're going to close you out at some horrible level. They say, "You didn't post the margin, we're going to close you out." And then what do you do? You're going to sue them? By the time this thing wends its way through the courts, you're out of business. And if you're being foreclosed on by a bank, and you're in litigation, that massively increases the probability that other banks will do the same thing to you, because they'll be worried, and you're caught in this vicious circle. Yeah, so, theoretically, in calm times you would look to the courts for vindication, but in difficult times the damage that's done may be irreversible before you can get any kind of remedy.

There was an interesting case back in 1998, some similar kinds of things happened. I recall that there was a hedge fund called High Risk Opportunities HUB Fund that had bought local ruble-denominated bonds in Russia, they were called GKOs. And they had hedged the currency risk with a French bank. And they were earning a spread between the rate on the treasury bills and the rate they were paying to hedge against ruble devaluation. So when the ruble did devalue, the French bank said, "Well, you know, there is a term in your hedge that says that if there is a convertibility event— in other words, the imposition of capital controls—then we don't need to pay you." And that was just complete bollocks, as far as I can tell. The documentation—it's funny, this bank tried to get us to do hedge business with them back then, so I think I got to see similar documentation, and we passed because the documentation was a little bit nonstandard—called for final settlement to be delayed until a convertibility event was resolved, but not for payment to be eliminated *tout court*. But in the meantime, this fund, it had leveraged the position, it had bought those treasury bills and borrowed money to pay for them—maybe it had put up 10 percent—and it had entered the hedge. And the idea is that if the ruble devalues, then the hedge counterparty has to pay the fund, and then that money would be used to pay their financing counterparties on the treasury bills to make up for the fact that the value of the treasury bills is dropping. But the French bank said, "No, we're not going to pay you." So they couldn't meet their margin calls on the treasury bills. They got blown out of those positions at these horrible levels, and the fund was basically out of business. And they sued, but it took years to go through the courts, and by then the fund was out of business.

n+1: Did they win the lawsuit?

HFM: In the end, you know, I'm not even sure. Because it took years, it was like *Jarndyce vs. Jarndyce*.

n+1: What would happen if they won? I mean, you win that lawsuit and you get your fund back?

HFM: No, your fund is done, right? Maybe then they have to pay out on the contracts. But by that time the losses that you've incurred are much worse than just the fact that you weren't paid the money you were owed on the contracts; it's like you don't have a business anymore, right? You just lost, you just got blown out the other side, and your ability to recover from that is limited. You just don't have a business anymore. Your reputation is damaged. And . . . let's say that situation by itself hadn't been enough to ruin the fund completely. If the fund's other counterparties see this is going on, they're saying, "Oh my gosh, this fund is in real trouble. I'm going to do whatever I need to do to withdraw my financing from that fund, because I don't want to suffer losses." So it would be enough to, you know, lead to the fund's failure.*

**n+1:** So you would come in very early. Why would it be guys in London who had information?

**HFM:** Just because of the time zones. I get in before most people in New York, and London is already actively trading, and as soon as people congregate, wherever it is, that's when the rumors start. They probably got the rumor from Asia, and it was passed on to London, passed on to New York.

**n+1:** So what do you do? How do you deal with that?

**HFM:** You wind up becoming a vector of the rumors, because you call up other places and say, "Hey, did you hear this rumor that X, Y, and Z, and what color do you have on that?" You're trying to gather as much pub as you can, but in reality it was a waste of time, because if a place is in crisis they're going to try to keep it under wraps, and it's

---

* High Risk Opportunities HUB Fund went into liquidation in the wake of the Russia crisis. Its liquidator sued the bank counterparties, claiming both the payments due under the hedge contracts and lost profits from the fund's having been forced into liquidation. The last claims were settled in 2007, nearly nine years after Russia's default. While the fund's creditors recovered on the order of 75 percent of their claims, investors in the fund were, as we say in the business, SOL: shit out of luck.

not like calling around, scouring your social network or your business network for gossip, is going to give you an accurate picture of what's going on.

But you have to feel that you're doing something.

**n+1:** But some of these places, they were going under, right?

**HFM:** Yeah, a few of them were. But there were many more false positives than false negatives. I mean, Lehman's collapse had definitely been announced a dozen times before it happened, and Bear's probably two dozen times, and, you know, Goldman Sachs's probably half a dozen times. Very few names were completely unsullied by these rumors.

**n+1:** Was it just these enormous places?

**HFM:** No, hedge funds. Hedge funds too.

+ + +

**n+1:** So these banks that tried to pull financing. Are you no longer friends with them?

**HFM:** With that part of the bank, sure, we won't do business with them. But there are other parts of the bank that we do business with. There's a certain amount of autonomy between business units.

**n+1:** And are you mad at those particular guys who went and did that . . . or are there not, you know, individual people involved in this?

**HFM:** They were people, and now they're wearing cement boots at the bottom of the East River.

**n+1:** I mean, when something like that happens.

**HFM:** Yeah, there's a lot of yelling and screaming. There are even swear words used.

**n+1:** Uh-huh. And you're mad at those particular guys, as opposed to the institution, or . . . ?

**HFM:** I'm mad at both. You're facing one or two people, right, and it's hard to know whether they're acting on their own initiative or whether they're being forced to do this by people above them, so it's hard to know exactly who to blame. My rule of thumb is I just yell at everybody.

**n+1:** But have you had situations where somebody behaved in that way and then, you know, a couple years later they resurfaced at some other bank, and they called you and said, "Hey, I'm sorry about that a few years ago, that was . . ."

**HFM:** That would be so much more upstanding than the way people actually behave. They call you up and they . . . you know what it's like? Were you picked on as a kid ever, like in elementary school?

**n+1:** No.

**HFM:** You weren't? Well, I was, and it's like I go back to the town I grew up in, you know, and I run into somebody, my main interaction with this guy is that he would pick me up and throw me into the garbage can in the girls' bathroom, okay?

**n+1:** [laughing]

**HFM:** For instance. And this was years ago, and now maybe he's pumping gas and I'm the hedge fund guy, right? And so you'd think he'd imagine I had some resentment or something, but, you know, he comes up and says, "Hey, it's great to see you!" You know, "We had such good times in school, didn't we? We should hang out sometime!"

It's much like that. It's like they can't live with themselves if they confront the fact that they've behaved atrociously and victimized people because it was convenient for them, and so they just create this alternate reality in their heads.

And so I have to say, "Are you kidding me? You tried to put me out of business three years ago! I would never deal with you!"

**n+1:** Does that happen often?

**HFM:** It tends to happen in difficult times. There certainly have been a number of cases where somebody who has treated me in a way that I've found to be really unfair resurfaces somewhere else and tries to behave as though it never happened. And if you call them on it, they go, "You know, it was my boss or my credit department or whatever." But this isn't a court, you're not innocent until proven guilty.

**n+1:** This person in your hometown, did they know that you've gone on to great success, or did they just happen to see you and they're like, "Oh, hey . . . you."

**HFM:** No, he just happened to see me. I don't know if he had any idea what's become of me, and I didn't drive up in a Ferrari wearing an Armani suit or anything. I was just grateful he didn't throw me into the garbage can, honestly.

+ + +

**n+1:** Can we talk about a fund that actually blew up, and this had consequences for you?

**HFM:** Well, no . . . there were very few funds that blew up that had consequences for me. Because in reality, in the end, hedge funds weathered this better than the banks. Hedge funds were much less leveraged than the banks.

And the liquidations were a lot more orderly than would have been the case for banks. You didn't have big, ugly, swampy bankruptcies like Lehman. Like one fund that went under was called Sowood. Which was ex–Harvard Management guys—they had been managers working for the endowment and then they went out and started their own fund, which had money from the Harvard endowment, among others. They had a fund, and it was a particular, you know, genre of trade that blew them up. It wasn't a particularly unwise trade; it was just something that was levered to an extent that seemed reasonable given the volatility of the trade in the past, but things kind of went haywire and then they were just, you know, out of business.

What did they do? It wasn't a swampy bankruptcy. They were too levered and it didn't work out for them. Another fund came in, looked at their books, and just bought the entire portfolio. At a level that pretty much wiped out the investors in Sowood. But it didn't inflict any losses on Sowood's trading counterparties or lenders or anything like that. The hedge fund community held up a lot better in some ways than the banks.

There's no government bailout for hedge funds. There really weren't too many instances where there were large losses that went beyond the investors in that fund, who are the people who are supposed to be taking the risk, right? The banks didn't suffer losses, significant losses, from lending to hedge funds.

**n+1:** And the guys who bought the fund, they weren't Yalies, were they?

**HFM:** No, I think Harvard, Citadel bought the Sowood assets. Citadel is owned by Ken Griffin . . . Harvard '89, I think. But anyway, Harvard's endowment had a bunch of money with Sowood.

**n+1:** And so how—

**HFM:** They used to work for the Harvard endowment, then they went and started their own shop. I could go on for a long time about the lunacy of these alums, most of them the class of '69, who complained about how much Harvard Management Company employees were paid. They chased away all this talent and Harvard wound up having to place the money with the funds that these guys started up. So they had the same people managing the money, only getting paid *more* and with less control and visibility for Harvard.

**n+1:** The class of '69 got together—because they're a bunch of hippies?

**HFM:** It's all fucking silly patchouli-stinking hippies from the class of '69 who probably spend their evenings listening to their Woodstock albums or whatever it is they do, and they are just upset about the fact that these people were getting paid a lot of money, but they were doing a very good job. As a result, they pushed all the talent out, and you see where the Harvard endowment has ended up because of it.

**n+1:** Where? I don't know.

**HFM:** Well, down 30 percent last year.*

**n+1:** Jeez. That's not good.

+ + +

**n+1:** Most of your fears at the time of the crisis were related to particular places blowing up and then worrying about your exposure?

**HFM:** We were worried about the stability of our financing, whether our counterparties would honor their commitments or whether they'd turn on us. And if they were turning on us, that didn't mean they had more ill will toward us or had any particular fear of us, because like I said we're very conservatively managed, but because they faced pressures of their own. They needed to get back capital from wherever they can, so they come to us and say, "You know I said I would commit financing to your mortgage bond positions for six months and so you'd have six months' notice if the terms of financing change, but fuck that, you need to give the money back now."

**n+1:** And when you're describing this chain that you would worry about late at night, you were worried that hedge fund A was blowing up, right?

**HFM:** It's usually good to start with a bank. You know, a bank fails and we have some exposure to that bank and so that means we lose

---

* For the fiscal year ending June 30, 2009, Harvard's endowment dropped 27.3 percent in value, the university announced at the end of September 2009. Unlike many hedge funds and banks, Harvard Management Company (HMC) has a compensation system for portfolio managers that includes clawbacks of previous years' bonuses in case of large losses, which, according to HMC, meant that "a substantial number of portfolio managers at HMC had portions of their bonuses earned in prior years 'clawed back' into the endowment." Perhaps this will warm the hearts of Harvard undergraduates as they eat their cold weekday breakfasts, hot breakfasts having fallen victim to budget cuts in 2009–10.

some of our cash, and some of that cash ends up getting vaporized
or gets frozen at that bank. And then that creates a concern among
other banks even though it doesn't really cause any trouble. You
know it's a loss, but it's a sustainable loss, but there's very little trust
in the market, and the other bank knows that the first bank is blowing up and they know that we must have exposure to them, so they
come in and they say, "You know what? I don't want to have any
more exposure to your fund." So they pull the financing and that
means our liquidity is even more stretched and maybe we need to
sell some assets to keep our liquidity at a level we consider to be safe.
And if we go out and do that, then people will say, "Oh these guys
are selling, so they must be in trouble, and so I need to pull my lines
from them and maybe some other funds at the same time," so everybody's trying to sell at the same time, which pushes prices down
and makes the trades you have in common with other funds perform
very poorly, which means that you're sustaining more losses, which
means more concern, and like ultimately the whole thing sort of
unwinds.

**n+1:** And did this happen to some extent?

**HFM:** It happened to *some* extent. But Lehman was the bank that
failed; it wasn't that there were four Lehmans. This nightmare scenario didn't occur.

We were not very leveraged, and a lot of other hedge funds were
also pretty prudently positioned. They had bad years, but they were
not to the point where they just went belly-up. I was a little bit surprised that there were as few ugly failures as there were.

**n+1:** We talked at the beginning of the year and I got the sense that
you were finding out how other hedge funds had done just kind of by
what other investors were saying to you. Do you know better now how
everybody did?

**HFM:** Yes. There are indices of hedge funds. The average was something like down in the mid-teens. But those indices tend to be a little bit misleading in that there's some survivorship bias, and there're some funds that stop reporting to the index or fall out, so it tends to overestimate performance. But there were some big funds that were down 20 and 30 and 40 percent. Some very well-regarded funds. Citadel—their main fund, I think, was down 55 percent. There were a few guys who made money, who were just positioned perfectly, but on the whole the sector put up very bad numbers. And there are many funds that lost a lot of money that, going forward, their business doesn't make a lot of sense, right? Because they need to make back what they've lost for their existing investors before they can start earning incentive fees again. So they're like, "This business doesn't make any sense. I'm going to have to pay my employees, and they're going to demand to get paid, but I have nothing to pay them with until I make 60 percent or something and get back to my high-water mark. So I'm just going to wind up the fund." There are a lot of funds that during this year have said that they're going off into the sunset, but it's on their own terms in a sense. Not because they've blown up or gone bankrupt; it's just because business there doesn't make sense anymore.*

**n+1:** Because of the weird kind of incentive structure?

**HFM:** It's an incentive problem. And it'll be interesting to see how investors try and deal with that incentive problem going forward. Because it's almost like you need to find a way to enslave the fund manager that just lost your money, that he has to work to try and make it back.

---

* Hedge fund closures actually seem to have hit a peak in 2008, with 1,471 liquidations, according to Hedge Fund Research, Inc. In the second quarter of 2009, the pace had slackened slightly: 292 funds liquidated in that period.

**n+1:** And so, during this high-pressure period, how long did this last?

**HFM:** The pressure went to a really intense pitch in the beginning of the third quarter, let's call it September, and it continued to feel that way until the end of January. At that point it started to feel like the worst, the heart attack, is over—you know, "We're not going to have a complete failure of the financial system." And the worries were more about, "Oh, what's the economic performance going to be like going forward? How are specific trades that I have on going to perform? How are specific borrowers going to be able to pay back their loans on time, or are we going to have to work on restructuring?" But during that autumn period, it was really more thinking about the survival of the whole financial system and whether the damage to the financial system was going to somehow cause our business specifically or more generally the hedge fund business to completely unravel. And then by January or February it was still very stressful, but it was really more relating to your own investments.

**n+1:** So during that high-pressure time did you make any mistakes?

**HFM:** The main mistakes were mistakes of omission. Toward the end of that high-pressure period there were some wonderful opportunities to take advantage of the dislocations, and for sure we were not aggressive enough. Because we were still traumatized by this whole financial system near-death experience. "Wow, this opportunity, in normal times, would be great, I would be all over this, but I don't want to take any risk, maybe we're going to slide back into that terrible crisis period."

And that is the same problem that happens every crisis. And every time the crisis passes, I'm like, "Gosh darn it, I missed it again. This was the opportunity of a lifetime! Next time when there's a crisis I'm going to tell myself, 'I've been through this before, the world's not going to end, and I'm going to pile in!'" But that's a very flawed way of thinking, a very emotional way of thinking. Because one of these crises—it may be the world will end.

**n+1:** You didn't panic at any point?

**HFM:** I panicked, but luckily my form of panic is deer in the headlights. It's hard to make too many errors of *com*mission if that's the way you panic. It might have saved me from selling things or taking positions off at the worst point. We managed to avoid that particular pitfall. And part of that was just that we were well positioned, we did have all of these locked-up financing arrangements that meant that we were never forced to unwind anything.

But we could talk about mistakes. The mistakes of commission generally don't take place in a crisis. They are the things that cause the crisis, the things that you do in the run-up, in the bubble years. I think that's true of most everybody in the financial market. The errors were the things they did in the good times.

+ + +

**n+1:** All right. Anything I'm missing from the recent things that are going on that you want to talk about?

**HFM:** Uh, I don't think so. I don't think so. Except I'll tell you this: I am considering retiring.

**n+1:** Well that'll be a . . . Holy—

**HFM:** Yeah. I don't know if I'm retiring entirely from finance forever, but I think from here and for a while. My fiancée and I, we've decided that we want to leave New York.

**n+1:** Whoa.

**HFM:** Yes.

**n+1:** Uh, what, and go where?

**HFM:** I think our first choice now is Austin.

**n+1:** [*laughs heartily*] That's where the slackers live.

**HFM:** Yes.

**n+1:** [*laughs quite a bit more*]

**HFM:** That's where the movie *Slacker* was filmed.

**n+1:** I know.

**HFM:** That's a great movie, I like that movie.

**n+1:** You want to move to Austin and become a slacker?

**HFM:** Well, I don't know if I want to become a slacker, but I want to move to Austin. I can't take another winter in New York, that's one thing. I have some financial reasons to go to a place where there's no state income tax, so I need to break away from New York, I'm getting killed on New York City taxes. And I want to go someplace where there's a university. I want someplace that's walkable. I want to go someplace where I know some people, and I do know some people in Austin. My fiancée's sister lives in Austin, so we know some people there. So that's the plan. I'm thinking it'd be nice to just retire, not do anything for a while. I don't know. Part of me's like, "You know what? I want to be done with finance. I've done everything I can do." The rewards are going to be a lot less going forward just because of regulation and taxes and stuff like that. And I'm not getting any younger, the men in my family don't have a long life expectancy, so you know . . .

n+1: What do you want to do at a university?

HFM: No, I mean there's more culture and interesting people there, in a university town.

n+1: Do you think, from our conversations, I've received enough training to take over your job?

HFM: I think you're ready as you'll ever be.

n+1: Fantastic.

HFM: I don't know, we'll see what happens. And maybe I will still do something from Austin, but it's hard to do the exact same job that I'm doing remotely. We have a good team, I could perform a less hands-on role—do only the broader portfolio strategy—but I don't want to be getting up at five in the morning and working until seven at night. It'll depend on what I ultimately decide and what my partners would agree to, and neither the decision nor the discussion have happened yet.

At a certain point you have to say, "I have enough." So if I'm working, it should be because I enjoy it. Otherwise, it's just like I'm being Scrooge McDuck, taking money that I'll never spend. Or it's like I'm motivated by *amour propre*. I need people to say that I'm a big hedge fund partner guy. And that's not a good reason either. The right question to ask myself is, "Am I still enjoying this?" And the answer is I'm finding it very stressful and a lot less enjoyable.

n+1: How much of that has to do with all the stuff that's been going on for the past few years?

**HFM:** Oh, a ton. It's not just last year—there have been many crises and many difficult junctures in my career—but if you've had that happen enough, you're just not resilient anymore. I found that even now that the worst of the crisis seems to be over, the day-to-day problems that I face that are just part and parcel of the job, I'm finding much more vexing than I used to. It's because I've used up my emotional resiliency.

**n+1:** [*pause*] I'm in shock.

**HFM:** It's not that surprising, is it?

**n+1:** Well, you—I thought you were going to go on vacation, and then you were going to, you know—

**HFM:** I went on vacation, and I didn't really miss this. At first I did; it was like withdrawal. By the end I was like, "Wow, this is great. I like not working."

**n+1:** [*laughs*] Well you know you're going to have to work. You're going to be bored—you can't just hike all the time and kayak.

**HFM:** I'm not sure that's true. People retire all the time.

**n+1:** When they're old.

**HFM:** [My friend] Gary's like, "You can't just become a consumer of stuff—intellectually and physically you can't." I'm like, "I'll take the other side of that bet, 'cause I think physically I can. I think it's quite possible."

**n+1:** Wow. [*pause*]

HFM: I gotta run.

n+1: Yes.

HFM: I have a squash match, so . . .

n+1: [laughs] Really?

HFM: Yeah.

n+1: That's more like it. That's the HFM I know and love.

# EPILOGUE

By the end of 2009, the U.S. economy had officially emerged from recession, and there were some positive consumer spending and financial indicators. Nonetheless, unemployment remained above 10 percent, and the housing market continued to slump. While most of the large banks repaid their TARP funds in time to avoid federal scrutiny of their year-end payment packages, bank lending, which had been the chief purpose of the TARP stimulus, remained depressed. The confirmation hearing of Ben Bernanke as the Chairman of the Federal Reserve was the most contentious such hearing in memory. Disgraced former New York governor Eliot Spitzer returned to the public stage, this time as an editorial writer, to harshly criticize the New York Fed for its kowtowing to Wall Street at the height of the crisis. Goldman Sachs, after public outcry over its banner 2009 year and proposed bonuses, made the decision to deliver the bonuses in the slightly less outrageous form of stock, rather than cash. And a Brooklyn jury acquitted the original Bear Stearns hedge fund managers, Ralph Cioffi and Matthew Tannin, of all charges. According to the *Daily News*, one juror said she would happily let the defendants invest her own money.

In short, things had more or less gone back to normal. The poor had grown poorer, while the rich had managed to survive.

In September, the coffee shop in Brooklyn where we did our first interview closed.

At the end of 2009, HFM left his hedge fund after more than a decade of nonstop work and bought a house in Austin, Texas.

# BIBLIOGRAPHY

This book went to press quite a bit later than many other books about the financial crisis, and so the interstitial summaries of events benefited from their reporting. The author of the summaries has in particular drawn on the following books:

William D. Cohan, *House of Cards: A Tale of Hubris and Wretched Excess on Wall Street* (Doubleday, 2009).

Michael Lewis, ed., *Panic: The Story of Modern Financial Insanity* (Norton, 2008).

Larry McDonald with Patrick Robinson, *A Colossal Failure of Common Sense: The Inside Story of the Collapse of Lehman Brothers* (Random House, 2009).

Andrew Ross Sorkin, *Too Big to Fail: The Inside Story of How Wall Street and Washington Fought to Save the Financial System—and Themselves* (Viking, 2009).

Gillian Tett, *Fool's Gold: How the Bold Dream of a Small Tribe at J. P. Morgan Was Corrupted by Wall Street Greed and Unleashed a Catastrophe* (Free Press, 2009).

**n+1** is a twice-yearly print journal of politics, literature, and culture. Founded in 2004, it has been praised by the *New York Times, TLS, Boston Globe*, and *Le Revue Des Deux Mondes*, and reviled by the *New Criterion* and *Gawker*. In 2006 it won the Utne Independent Press Award for Best Writing. An anthology of its most significant essays was published in 2008 by Suhrkamp, in German.

**Keith Gessen** is the author of *All the Sad Young Literary Men* and an editor and founder of *n+1*. He has written for *Dissent*, the *London Review of Books*, and *The New Yorker*.

**HFM** began his career in finance in the mid-1990s, on the emerging markets desk of a major hedge fund in New York. He now lives in Austin, Texas.

# INDEX

Note: Page numbers followed by an '*n*' refer to notes.

agriculture, 84–85

AIG
bailout of, 64, 77–79, 78*n*, 219
and bonuses scandal, 123, 141
credit rating of, 77, 78, 80
crisis at, 77–82
and investigation of payouts, 82*n*
management team of, 124
and potential fraud indictments, 147*n*

Argentina, 37, 42

auto companies
bankruptcy potential of, 66, 100–101
capacity of, 100
and car loans, 100, 217
and car sales, 84
and Cash for Clunkers program, 179
employment at, 217–18

Bankers Trust, 202–3

Bank of America
bailout of, 219
capitalization of, 169–70
and Countrywide acquisition, 138–39, 172
issues in, 138–39, 172
and Lehman, 63
and Merrill Lynch acquisition, 63, 123, 138–39, 172, 204, 205
reported profitability of, 134
and stress tests, 169–70

Bank of Japan, 130

bankruptcies
anticipation of, 56–57, 88
of Chrysler, 153, 161, 217
and debt collection, 158*n*, 160–61
effect on industries, 165–66
of Lehman Brothers, 63–64, 67–68, 70
potential for, in auto companies, 100–101
potential for, of Bear Stearns, 23, 33–34

banks
bailouts of, 35–36, 39, 44, 71*n*, 78–79, 78*n*, 134, 142, 153
bank runs, viii, 37, 116
and bankruptcy, 56–57, 65, 134, 218, 241 (*see also under* Lehman Brothers)
in Britain, 65
capitalization of, 29, 103, 169–70
cash hoarding of, 76
contractual agreements with, 230–34, 235–36
damage done to industry, 104*n*
and depositors, 136–37, 143
distress in, 26
executives of, 197–98
and FDIC deposit insurance, 75, 136, 139
and Glass-Steagall, 204
health of, 42, 54, 173, 184–85
hiring practices at, 228
lending of, 93, 104, 104*n*

and loss allocation, 46, 54–55
policies of, 223–28
regulation of, 227–28
reported profitability of, 134–35, 135n, 153
and stress tests, 137–38, 168–70
and TARP (see Troubled-Asset Relief Program)
zombie banks, 42–43, 44, 45–46, 136–37
See also specific banks
BarclayHedge, 41n
Bear Stearns
bailout of, 36, 71n
bank run, 38
capitalization of, 29
and credit default swaps, 39
crisis at, 23, 30–32, 33–34
and Federal Reserve, 29n, 33–36, 38–39, 42
and fraud charges, 146n
JPMorgan Chase's purchase of, 23, 29n, 31, 33, 202–3, 206
management team of, 23, 32, 198, 249
and mortgage-backed securities, 4
and rumors, 235
solvency of, 29, 29n
and write-downs, 27, 29
Bernanke, Ben, 64, 102n, 123, 249
black box trading (statistical arbitrage), 11–14, 18, 109–10, 112–13, 135
bonds, 104–5, 104n, 162–63
bonuses, 89, 96–97, 123, 141
Brazil, 104, 107–8, 165
breaking the buck, 64, 69–71
Britain, 65, 130
Bush administration, 4, 141

California, 3, 123, 210–13
capitalism, 148–49
Capital Purchase Program (CPP), 79n
Car Allowance Rebate System (CARS), 179, 217
Cassano, Joe, 147n
Cayne, Jimmy, 23, 198

CDOs (collateralized debt obligations), 10, 14–17, 18–19, 20
Chase Manhattan, 202, 204
Cheung, Meaghan, 106
China, 3, 52, 118, 125–29, 130, 132–33
Chrysler, 78, 153, 161, 217
Cioffi, Ralph, 30n, 146n, 249
Citadel, 239, 242
Citibank and Citigroup
bailout of, 79, 140n, 219
capitalization of, 44, 169
and compensation, 198
crisis at, 87, 138, 139–40
and government, 140n
issues in, 171–72
losses of, 27, 47
management team of, 36, 197
reported profitability of, 134
and Salomon Smith Barney, 206, 206n
and stress tests, 169, 171
as zombie bank, 136–37
Commerci, 107
commercial banks, 104n, 203, 204, 205–6
commercial paper market, 69–70, 74–75, 82, 103, 207
compensation of financial sector employees
and bonuses, 89, 96–97, 123, 141
at Citigroup, 140n
and clawbacks, 146, 240n
at Goldman Sachs, 184, 207
government reaction to, 141
at Harvard Management Company, 240n
in post-crisis financial sector, 228
salary levels, 147, 184, 198
construction industry, 118, 143–45, 145n, 218
consumer confidence, 216–17, 218
consumer spending, 28, 127, 147–49, 173, 184, 216
contractual agreements, 230–34, 235–36
corporate taxation, 175
Countrywide, 138, 172

credit
  availability of, 100, 104, 104*n*, 249
  deterioration of, 23
  system of, 219–23
credit default swaps, 39, 80, 82*n*
credit spreads
  about, 5*n*
  narrowing of, 134, 172, 215
  widening of, 55, 86, 102
Credit Suisse, 5*n*
criminalization of failure, 34, 187
Cuomo, Andrew, 123
currency hedges, 107–8

Daschle, Tom, 123
Dean Witter, 205
debt collection, 157–61, 158*n*
Dimon, Jamie, 203, 204
dollar, 6–8, 17–18, 51–53, 116–17,
  129–32

economy. *See* real economy
Einhorn, David, 81
emerging markets, 47, 53, 141, 148, 151,
  188
emotion in trading, 45, 135, 247
Enron scandal, 186, 186–87*n*
equity markets, 134, 163, 172, 173, 215
ethical issues, 150, 151–52
euro, 52, 130, 131–32
European Monetary Union, 130–32
Exchanged Stabilization Fund, 65
exchange rates, 132
exports, 51–52, 53, 127, 128, 130

Fannie Mae
  insolvency of, 50, 50*n*
  reported losses, 55, 153, 207
  rescue of, 47, 63, 67
Federal Deposit Insurance Corporation
  (FDIC), 47, 57, 75, 103, 114, 139
Federal Reserve
  and AIG, 64, 78*n*
  balance sheet of, 75–76, 215
  and Bear Stearns, 29*n*, 33–36, 38–39,
    42

chairman position of, 102, 102*n*
on commercial bank lending, 104*n*
and commercial paper, 65, 74–75,
  103, 207
effectiveness of actions of, 218–19
and Fannie Mae and Freddie Mac
  rescue, 47
interest rates cuts of, 3
and market liquidity, 218
and Merrill Lynch's acquisition of
  Bank of America, 205
money creation by, 75–76, 215
and short-term credit market, 65, 103
and Treasury bonds, 5*n*
financial sector
  and government response to crisis,
    218
  mood in, 134, 215
  power of, 141
  profits in, 184
  qualifications of personnel in, 98, 99
  recovery in, 179, 207
  risk tolerance in, 172
Florida, 3, 44
foreclosures, 51, 58, 105–6, 118, 153,
  207
fraud, 146, 146–47*n*, 151–52
Freddie Mac
  insolvency of, 50, 50*n*
  reported losses, 55, 153, 207
  rescue of, 47, 63, 67
front-running, 110–11
Fuld, Richard, 123
funds-of-funds, 111–12

GE Capital, 104–5
Geithner, Timothy, 63, 102
Glass-Steagall, 204
Goldman Sachs
  and AIG, 77, 82*n*
  as bank holding company, 65
  compensation and bonuses at, 184,
    207
  influence of, in government, 141, 142
  as investment bank, 64, 206
  reported profitability of, 134, 153

and rumors, 235
and statistical arbitrage, 12
status of, 202, 203
talent at, 142
and TARP, 179
Greenspan, Alan, 65–66
Griffin, Ken, 239
gross domestic product (GDP), 51, 51n, 184

Harvard Management Company, 238–40, 240n
hedge funds
about, 41–42
closures of, 242, 242n
damage done to industry, 40–41, 41n, 45–46
liquidations in, 238
and Madoff scandal, 111–12
managers of, 9
and penalties for failure, 195
performance of, 94–95, 175–77, 238, 241–42
reaction to the bailout, 142
redemptions in, 56, 72–74, 94–95, 156
risk aversion in, 55–56
and rumors, 235
and short-term credit market, 72
and staffing, 177, 200
stress associated with, 150–52
and subprime mortgages, 14–15, 18
trades in, 93
and year-end closing, 91–92
Highbridge, 12
High Risk Opportunities HUB Fund, 232–34, 234n
hotel industry, 213–14
housing market
and construction industry, 218
continued slump in, 249
decline in home prices, 4
and demand for houses, 100, 210
deterioration of, 93
foreclosures in, 51, 58, 105–6, 118, 153, 207

housing boom, 3–4
and labor market, 216
and loss allocation, 58–59, 143–45

Iceland, 65
illegal laborers, 118, 145n
imports, 130
IndyMac, 47, 57
inflation, 75, 116, 117, 130, 174, 219
insider trading, 108, 147n
interest rate swaps, 108
International Monetary Fund, 130, 135n
Internet boom and bubble correction, 3, 98–99, 119
investing, lack of, 76–77
investment banks
in Brazil and Mexico, 108
competition in, 184–85
and Glass-Steagall, 204
individual fates of, 202–6
and punishment of financial executives, 186
regulation of, 107
risks held by, 27
and subprime mortgages, x, 3
See also specific banks
Ireland, 115

Japan, 42–43, 45–46
J. P. Morgan, 202, 203
JPMorgan Chase
and Bear Stearns, 23, 29n, 31, 33, 202–3, 206
health of, 138
management team of, 204
and TARP, 179
and Washington Mutual, 65

labor market
and auto companies, 217–18
effect of financial crisis on, 96–97
effect on recovery of, 218
and job loss, 51, 83
as lagging indicator, 215, 216
and layoffs, 66, 95, 124

labor market (*cont.*)
  resource misallocation in, 145, 145*n*
  and skill sets, 145–46
  *See also* unemployment
Latin America, 148
Lehman Brothers
  commercial paper, 71, 71*n*
  crisis at, 38–39, 38*n*
  failure of, 63–64, 67–68, 70, 77,
    204–5, 206
  HFM's exposure to, 156
  leadership of, 123
  losses of, 47
  and moral hazard issue, 68
  and Reserve Primary Fund, 70, 70*n*,
    71*n*, 77
  and rumors, 235
Lewis, Ken, 123, 205
LIBOR-OIS spread, 173*n*
Liquid Universe Corporate Index
  Spread over Benchmark, 5*n*
Long-Term Capital Management,
  193–95, 193–94*n*, 199, 200, 202
losses and loss allocation
  in banking sector, 46, 47, 135*n*
  bearers of, 43–44
  distribution of, 141
  extent of, 49–50, 55
  in housing sector, 58–59, 143–45
  importance of loss recognition, 64
  in Japan, 45–46
  original creation of, 58
  process of loss allocation, 43, 54–55,
    57*n*, 136–37

Madoff, Bernard
  implications of scheme, 111–12
  indictment of, 89, 147*n*
  insiders' suspicions of, 109–11
  SEC investigation of, 106
  sentencing of, 179, 185–86
Madoff, Ruth, 124
margins on derivatives, 223–28
market-making operations, 110–11
mark-to-market, 23
Meriwether, John, 194–95, 199

Merrill Lynch
  and Bank of America merger, 63, 123,
    138–39, 172, 204, 205
  bonuses given at, 89
  capitalization of, 44
  and Enron scandal, 186, 186–87*n*
  as investment bank, 206
  losses of, 23, 27, 47
  management team of, 23, 36, 89, 198
Mexico, 104, 107–8
money market funds, 69–72, 103
moral hazard issue, 36, 68
Morgan Stanley, 64, 65, 206, 206*n*
Morgan Stanley Dean Witter, 202, 205
mortgages
  compared to Ponzi schemes, 222–23
  and extent of financial crisis, 50
  and foreclosures, 51, 58, 105–6, 118,
    153, 207
  packaging and selling of, 3, 4, 15, 16,
    17, 18, 143
  remaining problems in, 173
  *See also* subprime mortgages
municipal and state governments,
  101–2, 107–8

nationalization, 64, 87*n*, 136, 141, 142,
  171

Obama, Barack, 65, 75, 102*n*, 113, 153,
  161
Obama administration, 141, 174–75, 179
O'Neal, Stan, 23

Pandit, Vikram, 138, 140*n*
Paulson, Henry, 4, 34, 64, 65, 123
performance analysis, 175–77
Ponzi schemes, 110, 147*n*, 222–23
populist rage, 124, 153
presidential campaign, 64–65
private lending, 162, 163–67, 168
public relations, 158, 159

quantitative trading, 11–12, 199–202

rating agencies, 10–11, 15, 143

real economy
  and bankruptcies, 166
  contraction of, 217
  in early stages of crisis, 51
  effects of financial crisis on, 88, 105, 118
  financial sector's relationship with, 82–83
  and loss recognition, 58
  recession in, 51, 51n, 52n, 117, 218, 249
  recovery of, 173–74, 179, 215, 216, 218–19
  sluggish performance of, 45, 207
real estate market, 27, 164–65
recession, 51, 51n, 52n, 117, 218, 249
regulatory system, 35, 57, 106, 205–6, 227–28. See also Federal Reserve
relationships, professional, 235–37
relative value trade, 192–93
researching investments, 189–93
reserve currency status, 129–32
Reserve Primary Fund, 64, 69–71, 69n, 70n, 71n, 77
resource misallocation
  of financial resources, 99
  and loss allocation, 43, 58
  and pay scale for finance, 97
  of people resources, 97, 99, 143
  of productive capacity, 100
  and recovery process, 173
  as source of crisis, 83, 85
risk taking and risk management
  aversion to, 55–56, 85–86, 104n, 243
  basic assumptions in, 28
  capacity for risk taking, 29
  effect of write-downs on, 29
  exchange rate analogy for, 72
  and fund failures, 195
  and lack of available credit, 55
  post-crisis trends in, 172
  risk disclosure, 107–8
  in subprime market, 16–17, 27
Robertson, Julian, 6–7, 9
Roubini, Nouriel, 217
rumors, 229–30, 234–35
Russia, 45, 65, 130, 164–65, 181, 203

S&P 500, 65, 83, 207
salaries. See compensation of financial sector employees
Salomon Brothers, 195, 199, 206
Salomon Smith Barney, 202, 206
Sarbanes-Oxley, 34
SDR (special drawing right), 130–31
Securities and Exchange Commission (SEC), 106–9
short-term credit, 70, 72, 82, 84, 103, 207
short-term money markets, 173
sit-in at Chicago window factory, 66
Soros, George, 9
Sowood fund, 238, 239
Spitzer, Eliot, 187
split-strike conversions, 110
Standard & Poor's, 143
Stanford, Allen, 147n
State Street, 179
statistical arbitrage (black box trading), 11–14, 18
sterling, 130, 131
stimulus programs, 75, 87n, 113–17, 174–75, 219
strategic default, 158–59
stress tests, 137–38, 168–70
subprime mortgages
  and beginning of the financial crisis, 4
  Bush on, 4
  and Countrywide, 138, 172
  damage from, 23
  delinquency rate in, 46, 46n
  and demand for CDO paper, 15–17, 20
  experts in, 19–22
  and extent of financial crisis, 50
  and hedge funds, 14–15, 16–17, 18, 93
  and housing market, 93
  junior and senior tranches in, 93
  loss allocation in, 50
  risk in, 16–17, 27
  short sales in, 10–11
  warning signs in, 20–21
  and write-downs, 27–28, 27n, 28n, 29
Summers, Larry, 102

SunTrust, 170
supply chains, 84–85

Tannin, Matthew, 30n, 146n, 249
taxes, 150, 175
Tenner, Edward, 115
Tett, Gillian, 4
Thain, John, 198
transparency, 54, 56
Tribune Corp, 83, 83n
Troubled-Asset Relief Program (TARP)
  and AIG, 78n
  effectiveness of, 218
  fiscal impact of, 79n
  initial response to, 64
  as investment, 78–79, 78n
  and mortgage crisis, 105
  purpose of, 75, 103
  repayment of funds, 179, 249
  vote on, 65, 86–87, 229

UBS, 23
unemployment
  in early stages of crisis, 51
  effect on recovery of, 216, 218
  and financial sector, 83, 88

high levels of, 117n, 207, 215, 249
  of the late seventies, 117
  and real estate crisis, 118
U.S. Department of the Treasury
  and AIG, 78n
  and Bank of America merger, 205
  and Bear Stearns, 34, 38–39, 42
  effectiveness of actions of, 218–19
  and money market fund guarantee, 65
  proposed intervention of, 54
  secretary of, 102
and TARP, 179

Wachovia, 139
Wall Street, 206
Washington Mutual, 65
Wells Fargo, 138, 139, 170, 171

yen, 130, 131

Zell, Sam, x, 83n
Zillow, 106
zombie banks, 42–43, 44, 45–46,
  136–37
zombie companies, 44, 50
ZUNK bonds, 189–91